THE
HOUSEMATES

THE
HOUSEMATES

EVERYTHING ONE STUDENT LEARNT ABOUT LOVE, CARE AND DEMENTIA FROM LIVING IN A NURSING HOME

TEUN TOEBES

With Jonathan de Jong

Translated by Laura Vroomen

1 3 5 7 9 10 8 6 4 2

First published in 2023 by September Publishing

First published in the Netherlands in 2021 by De Arbeiderspers, Amsterdam, with the title *VerpleegThuis*

This book was published with the support of the Dutch Foundation for Literature.

N **ederlands**
letterenfonds
dutch foundation
for literature

Teun Toebes wrote *The Housemates* in close collaboration with documentary maker and author Jonathan de Jong.

Front cover photo, Teun and Eugenie: Annabel Oosteweeghel
Back cover photo, Teun with (from left to right) Jeanne, Ad, Juul, Elly, Eugenie, Tineke and Petra: author's own

Typeset by RefineCatch Limited, www.refinecatch.com
Printed in Poland on paper from responsibly managed, sustainable sources by Hussar Books

ISBN 9781914613395
Ebook ISBN 9781914613401

September Publishing
www.septemberpublishing.org

'Life here has no purpose, and when you no longer matter you might as well be dead'

Muriëlle Mulier – housemate

Dementia in numbers

- In the UK, there are 944,000 people estimated to be living with dementia; this is due to increase to 1.6 million by 2050.[1]
- Dementia cost the UK economy an estimated £25 billion in 2021.[2]
- In the USA, of those at least 65 years of age, there were an estimated 5 million adults with dementia in 2014, with projections to be nearly 14 million by 2060.[3]
- In the US, in 2023, dementia will cost the nation US$345 billion (this does not include the value of unpaid caregiving).[4]
- Globally, more than 55 million people have dementia. This will increase by 10 million each year.[5]
- In 2019, dementia cost economies globally US$1.3 trillion (about 50 per cent of these costs are attributable to care provided by informal carers).[6]

Contents

THE HOUSEMATES

Preface

My name is Teun Toebes and I believe that people living with dementia don't get the care and attention they deserve. It makes me incredibly sad. Not only because I love my housemates with dementia dearly, but even more so because this could be my future if I ever receive the diagnosis myself. After a life of freedom and self-determination, who'd want to end up in a system of indignity and exclusion? Who'd want to spend his or her final years as someone who's no longer seen as an individual, but as one of a group of sick people who've lost the plot? Who'd look forward to living in a home where the long corridors echo with loneliness and the TV blaring in the lounge is the only sign of life? Do you fancy such a future for yourself? I didn't think so! It has to change and that's why I've written this book.

The Housemates is a heartfelt indictment, not against the care sector, but against the way our society views people with dementia. Is it a devastating indictment? Absolutely, because life in a nursing home is devastating – it's something I encounter every day.

This isn't *the* truth; this is *my* truth and I admit it can be confrontational at times. But I hope my story will lead to dialogue and new insights, so that together we can make some much-needed improvements to the care we provide for people with dementia. We need to show that those living with dementia can still have a meaningful life; once we realise this as a society, the nursing home – my home – will have a hopeful future.

A better future sounds good, of course, but what's the situation like right now? When you're diagnosed with a form of dementia today, you go down a medical pathway with a great deal of attention placed on 'the patient' and lots of discussions *about* you. You'll live at home for as long as possible, until your condition deteriorates and it's no longer viable for either medical or social reasons. Or until your carer, often your partner, breaks down. The next step is a nursing home, where you'll find yourself in a mini society with all the hallmarks of a totalitarian regime. Did I really just say that? Yes, and I mean it, but like everybody who works in the care sector, I say this with the best of intentions. To my mind, the fact that the nursing home is set up in such a way as to exert *total* control over my life and that of my housemates means that it bears little or no resemblance to a democratic and equal society.

Just to be clear: I'm not writing this to make things difficult for my colleagues in the care sector or to portray them as a bunch of careless pencil pushers – far from it. I actually want them to have the freedom to change the way they think and act, and to discuss among themselves *how* care is provided and, above all, *why* it's done in the way it is now. That's what I'd like to achieve with this book. As a young care assistant, I'm so frustrated by the inhumane treatment of people with dementia today that my motivation to do this work is melting away like snow in the sun.

As much as we try to give loving care, as providers we appear to have lost sight of the essence. The current system is undermining lasting human relationships and is moving towards a model of medicalisation that fails to adequately see individuals for who they are. It looks as if it's almost all about money, appointments and expertise, and we're losing track of the people we're supposed to be looking after. I believe that we need to be attentive to the wishes of individuals with dementia and that the care for these people must – and can – change.

If we want to implement real change and humanise care, we must start by asking ourselves the fundamental question: what does it mean to live with dementia?

With that question in the back of my mind, over a

year ago, I moved into a nursing home. This allowed me to experience life with dementia from a range of different perspectives: as a nurse and as a student of Care Ethics and Policy, but, above all, as a human being. My housemates and I have created special memories together and a dynamic and loving relationship. With them, I feel that I experience the crux of human existence.

It's truly wonderful to be able to call this environment my home. I feel privileged to learn from these fine people and to discover more about their inner world. But most amazing of all is that every day I get to share in the happiness of people who in the eyes of society are incapable of being happy.

That's why I dedicate this book to those who are so often forgotten: people living with dementia.

I

SEEING THE LIGHT

My heart's been stolen

'If you're talking to Teun, it's bound to be about dementia,' those around me have a habit of saying. Every day, I get asked where my passion for people with dementia comes from. And no wonder, as it's not exactly a topic you'd expect to come up at an average twenty-two-year-old's birthday party.

Everybody assumes that dementia runs in the family, and it does, but that was certainly not what first drew me to it. My interest was piqued on a work placement during my nursing course. I ended up on the secure unit of a nursing home dedicated to people living with dementia. I must confess that it was a lot to take in, as what I saw didn't exactly correspond to the idea I had when I enrolled in the degree.

Perhaps I was a bit naïve, but, like many, I grew up with US television series about handsome doctors and young nurses who save the world while busy dating each other. Of course, I knew that this portrayal of the care sector wasn't entirely accurate, but the reality was such a let-down that I wanted to call it quits straightaway. Those people who sat around long tables staring into space all day made me feel uneasy. Was *this* my future, I wondered? What difference could I possibly make in this dreary world behind closed doors?

As sweet as my mother usually is, there are times when she's unexpectedly feisty and tough. When she heard me moan about my degree choice, she told me in no uncertain terms that quitting wasn't really an option. 'Good care can only be provided by caring people and if there's one thing I know, my boy, it's that you're one of them.' Although I was well aware that my mother, who works in the care sector herself, is more than a little biased, I took the compliment and, a week later, I went back to the ward with some healthy misgivings.

I had a look around, chatted a bit and had the odd cup of tea. Then I suddenly realised something that, as an adolescent boy, I really didn't want to: my mother was right! Right from the off, I enjoyed my contact with the residents, especially when I met John Francken, a former construction foreman. It was because of him that I grew to love the care sector as well as people with dementia, and not just him. He showed me, a seventeen-year-old, that as a society, we don't properly understand 'the nursing home resident' because we just don't want to accept that 'they', in their own remarkable interior world, have exactly the same needs as 'we' have in the outside world.

'Listen up, Teun,' John said. 'My whole life, I got treated normally, until the doctor said: "You've got Parkinson's." It was all downhill from there, not so much with me, but more with the way people behaved towards me and talked about me. The contact with my old workmates changed, neighbours looked at me differently because they felt sorry for me and I was constantly being asked if I was all right. So basically, my life as a normal person was over . . . And I don't blame them, pal, because nobody on the outside knows anything about this bloody disease. But what I do mind, Teun,' he continued, 'is how I'm treated *in here*, where it's full of people who have something wrong with them and who bloody well know it. You'd expect the staff to recognise that we're not barmy, that we're not all the same or at the same stage of the illness. Shouldn't we be normal in here, of all places? But they're treating me like I'm bonkers, like I don't know what I'm doing, don't matter anymore. They forget that the man they're looking at is John Francken, and that this man has had a good life and used to enjoy the little things – a bit of banter, a joke, or even just people walking past the building site with a spring in their step. They forget that this very same man still loves all that, even if I'm confused sometimes and I forget things. I may be forgetful, but from the day I moved in here, pal, they've forgotten about *me*, not the other way round . . .'

Gulp. For a moment, we looked at each other, speechless and with tears in our eyes. For a moment, there was no tough guy sat opposite me, but a human being with the sweetest yet saddest expression I'd ever seen. Then I cleared my throat and said gently: 'I won't be doing that, John. I won't forget you, I promise.'

Because of that promise, I felt I had something to prove to John, and that is that as a society we *can* listen to him and the thousands of others living with dementia. And so John not only became my buddy, but the inspiration behind my mission to improve the quality of life for people with dementia. And that mission began right there and then.

In my free time, I'd go out for ice cream with John. We'd laugh at some of his rather sexist 'builders' jokes' and race around the village in my car, insofar as that was possible in that old rust bucket of mine. And, as the icing on the cake, yours truly, a somewhat vain nurse-in-the-making, was the only person on the ward allowed to trim John's moustache. Perhaps not that great an honour on the face of it, but anyone who knew John would understand. John not only taught me to really look and listen to people with dementia, he also showed me something I hadn't been able to see during my first visit: the human being behind the illness.

A second reason for wanting to help people with dementia came several years later, when my grandmother's younger sister, Greet, was diagnosed with Alzheimer's, the most common form of dementia. I remembered Greet from my grandma's milestone birthdays, when she'd be the one moaning and complaining about other people. I also recalled that she was always dressed to the nines, wearing pearls. Greet had been alone for much of her life: her husband had died young, leaving her involuntarily childless. To have something to care for, Greet got herself two pooches – a couple of lapdogs, or 'yap dogs' as she called them. Every year, she had their portraits taken, both of them wearing a red bow, and gave the smartly framed photograph pride of place on her wall.

Greet had little or no contact with the rest of the family, but as she got older she developed a closer bond with my aunt, her niece. When Greet was diagnosed with Alzheimer's disease – after a long period of shame and concealing her symptoms – my aunt became her legal guardian and was given lasting power of attorney over Greet. At the time, I didn't give it a second thought, but it's a formality that epitomises what your life is like from that moment on: a life without an official voice, free will or self-determination. A life in which you're legally no longer heard, simply because you don't have the right to speak, whatever you say. Perhaps it's this stroke of the pen that's inadvertently at the root of how, as a society, we view people with dementia.

The moment she was diagnosed, Greet began to withdraw even further. Her blinds remained resolutely shut and the meals she received from relatives were immediately passed on to the dogs – their welfare was paramount to her. But sometimes she'd forget that besides dementia she also had diabetes, a combination that can be dangerous, as we found out when the police had to force entry twice while Greet was unconscious on the floor. It became clear that it was no longer safe for her to live at home, in the house where she'd lived her whole life. That came as a huge shock because her autonomy was perhaps most precious to her – not surprising when you think that for much of her life she'd had to fend for herself. But after a good conversation with my aunt, Greet agreed that her safety was at stake. With hindsight, she might have chosen to accept that risk rather than go along with what was in store for her.

All that was needed now was a court order to set the move to a nursing home in motion, which followed soon after. Maybe it was because there was family involved or because this was the first time I saw how people ended up in a nursing home, but I couldn't stop thinking about the fact that a woman was forced to leave her house after fifty-eight years. What must that feel like, especially when you don't always understand *why* you had to leave? It's no wonder that most people are terrified when they move into a nursing home, something that never fails to hit a nerve with me. Surely there has to be another way? Even in terms of design and layout, a nursing home is so different from a private dwelling that residents rarely, if ever, feel at home. That is not to say that nursing homes should be abolished, because remaining at home wasn't an option for Greet. But living in fear shouldn't be either.

As chance would have it, I worked in the nursing home that Greet moved into. Hand in hand, we entered the living area, where she sat down on the chair closest to the window. That turned out to be no coincidence. 'Right, this spot is mine, boy. At least I get to choose something in here,' she said cynically, as her eyes drifted to the fenced-off garden.

I soon became my great-aunt's point of contact for anything care related. It was an unusual dual role: one moment I was a healthcare professional, the next I provided care out of love for my relative. And the good thing was that she also took care of *me*. She could sense when I was busy or struggling with something and she would always give me tailor-made advice. It was fascinating to see that she could read me so well and it once again confirmed my suspicion that not only can you connect with someone with dementia, but you can establish a lasting and reciprocal relationship too – even if you have to go about it differently. This took a while to sink in because it wasn't at all what I'd learnt on my course. My realisation set something off in me, which further strengthened my intention to improve the quality of life for people like my great aunt.

To me, the two separate roles of official care provider and informal carer were complimentary, if difficult at times. Not least when I was consulted about major decisions, such as how long we'd want to continue medical treatment if her symptoms worsened. Such questions are tough for any twenty-year-old care assistant, but even more so when your own family is involved. Being an informal carer was totally new to me and, like so many others, I was trying my hardest. The personal care, on the other hand, didn't take any getting used to. To my surprise, I felt privileged rather than awkward about taking physical care of Greet, and luckily Greet felt the same way. Before I could even hand her a washcloth, she'd already dropped her trousers and said: 'Wash me, Teun.' In no time, we'd established a strong bond and she'd often refer to me as 'her boy'. But, proud as she was, she could look very jealous whenever I gave attention to her fellow residents.

In the months that followed, she changed from an unkempt and embittered woman into the lady I recognised from the parties in the old days. She looked chic again and was always over the moon when the dogs, her 'woofies', came to visit. Her character had remained virtually unaffected by the dementia, though, so she could still grumble with the best of them. When it came to her day-to-day freedom of choice or when something wasn't to her liking, she could make things pretty difficult for the nursing staff on duty.

Most people won't bat an eyelid when they read this next sentence, but I've chosen my words carefully as they capture the reality of care to a T: when people with dementia push back, they're almost immediately branded 'difficult'. Consequently, many 'difficult' people are sedated to the point of coma. Because, let's face it, isn't having a conversation with or offering a sympathetic ear to someone living with dementia basically pointless . . .?

This situation really pains me because why would diagnosis with a form of dementia determine whether a person can be happy or not? Why would such a diagnosis condemn you to hours of listening to André Rieu in the lounge when you've always loved the Rolling Stones and this kind of saccharine music – no disrespect, André – isn't your cup of tea? Why does it result in flower arranging when you hate gardening, or listening to yet another choir that's come to sing old, sentimental ballads when you'd much rather play Whitney Houston or the Beastie Boys in your room? Please explain to me why a diagnosis justifies this kind of approach and, above all, why it means that when you stand up for yourself, you're robbed of your voice, either medicinally or through other measures? It doesn't just sound daft, it *is* daft! In what kind of world do you get punished for standing up for yourself? Sadly, this was the everyday reality for John, later for Greet and, to my immense regret, for many others to this day.

This is not an attack on care providers but an indictment of a system that has created a huge distance between people with dementia and the rest of society. This system has not only made laws that say that people with dementia may be marginalised – and ignored when it comes to fundamental or personal matters – but it has also created a corresponding climate of care in which such marginalisation isn't the exception but the rule. This system is the reason why nothing is changing, because once the absurd has been rendered normal through policy, you can't expect those working in the care sector to defy the rules. Anyone who does tends to be seen as 'difficult' and that . . . that is something nobody wants.

As the months went by, Greet's health declined. She was confused more often and would wonder where her parents were. I could feel her pain when she told me that her parents had passed away, but she'd been unable to attend their funeral. Or so she thought. As her brain deteriorated, so did her body. She often complained of pain for which she received medication, but the side effects meant she slept for much of the day. Slowly, her lungs began to give out. She wheezed as she clutched the humidifier.

After several weeks, during which the proud woman I'd come to know again had been increasingly absent, I received a call from one of the carers. Greet was in a bad way, would I come in to take a decision? After consulting with the doctor and the care coordinator, I called my aunt, her legal guardian, and suggested to her that it might be better to withdraw life-sustaining treatments. In our view, Greet's suffering was no longer proportional to the better moments, so death would be a release for her. But it was a tough decision. Greet herself could no longer tell us what she wanted because she was in a deep sleep. My aunt backed the decision and I drove over to my grandma to inform her that the last remaining member of the family she grew up with was going to die. She was behind the decision all the way and together we made our way back to the nursing home.

Soon after, the moment came to start palliative sedation, which involves administering medication to put someone in a deeper sleep and relieve suffering. In principle, a person can still wake up when the medication is withdrawn before their heart stops beating. My grandma was astonished when we explained this to her: 'Why doesn't it just end when you give that medication? Why leave someone to wither away for days?' I nodded because I understood where she was coming from. They're often very long and strange, those days of waiting while someone is dying. You can sense it. The atmosphere in the room is simultaneously ominous and heavenly. You find yourself in a kind of surreal no-man's-land where every now and again, you're brought back down to earth by gurgling breaths that come at ever-increasing intervals. Some people find this period restful because it provides an opportunity for an extended goodbye, but I was hoping Greet would quickly get to the other side. I brought my head close to hers one last time to thank her for allowing me to get to know her again. 'Rest in peace,' I whispered in her left ear, after which my grandma bid her sister farewell in her own way. 'Bye girl,' she said lovingly.

With a colleague by my side, I took the syringe with morphine and the appropriately named sedative Dormicum and slowly injected the fluid via a needle in Greet's chest into her body. Two nights later, my mother woke me. It was done; her heart had stopped beating.

In the months that followed, I missed her terribly. Every day I wondered whether I'd given her the best possible life at the nursing home or if I'd been too blinded by acquired patterns of behaviour that had made my great aunt a 'patient'. But the more I thought about it, the more convinced I became that I'd always seen Greet for who she was – that eccentric person with both good and bad qualities that I loved more and more every day – and not my sad great aunt with dementia. This filled me with hope. The 'reimagining' of patients into individuals seemed so easy to me that the future of caring for people with dementia looked a great deal brighter.

To test whether creating a better and more humane care sector is indeed as simple as that, I decided to raise my mission to a higher level by not only caring for people with dementia but by living with them as well. As in, actually moving into a nursing home? Exactly. A more inclusive society begins at home.

An open mind

As a care provider, I know that many nursing homes have empty rooms because for years – for a variety of reasons – there's been a shortage of staff to look after residents. That's the sad reality and, given the rising tide of people with dementia, it's only going to get worse in the future.

Our expectations of nursing home care play a big part in this. We tend to interpret the word 'care' too literally, as we're under the illusion that it takes mostly medically trained personnel to make people with dementia feel at home. That's not the case. When I see how visitors, residents' family members and my own friends treat the people living here, I can't help but conclude that as care providers, we have a lot to learn from them. They tend to have the same instinctive, open-minded approach I see in colleagues who have just finished their training and who give their all to establishing a connection. Unfortunately, it usually doesn't take long for these newcomers to trade in their enthusiasm for a mere box-ticking exercise. It's very upsetting to me because caring for people is something you do with your heart, not with pen and paper. The fact that regulations are putting a dampener on enthusiasm and warmth really is the bane of today's policy and the deathblow to humane care. People just want to be treated normally. That's why it's time for us all to be more proactive; if we continue in this vein, humane care will remain a pipe dream.

So, one Monday afternoon in March, I plucked up the courage to pitch my idea of living in a nursing home to the entire board of a care organisation. Their professed core values were 'attention, positivity and professionalism' so, as an enthusiastic youngling, I thought: this is the place for me!

Ahead of the interview, I'd given a lot of thought to what it was that I wanted to contribute to the organisation and to the lives of the residents with dementia, my future housemates. I thought it would be incredibly edifying to experience what it's like to live in a nursing home – for both myself and the organisation – and I wanted to start from these two key principles:

1. As a resident in the nursing home, I have no professional status within the organisation; that's to say, I'm not a nurse and I'm not expected to carry out nursing duties. This

makes it possible for the relationship between me and my housemates to remain on an equal footing.

2. I have complete journalistic freedom, so as long as the residents consent to sharing their experiences, I can write what I want and even make videos with them. Social media is an excellent way of introducing society to people living with dementia. It reduces the gap between the two.

It soon became clear that my dream would come true! I was allowed to go and live in one of the nursing homes. A room would be available for me within the next few months.

When I went to meet the two managers of the home I'd be moving into, the floor supervisor was initially a little taken aback by the idea. I don't blame her. If I'd been in her situation, I'd have had plenty of questions too. But when we talked, both managers turned out to be open to new ideas. They told me that they also believed that the care sector had to change, so we were a perfect match for one another.

I was over the moon as I joined the floor supervisor to meet my future housemates. I was immediately struck by the scale of the building. It had an intricate system of corridors across two floors and an entrance the size of a shopping centre. The colour scheme of the various apartments stood out too: green, blue and orange. I was hoping for a place in one of the latter, as it's my favourite retro shade. My wish became reality: team orange it was. Talk about getting off to a good start.

One by one, I got to know my housemates, which was not unlike meeting fellow students in a hall of residence. Would they like me and accept me in their midst? The first to introduce herself was Leny, who studied me briefly and then commented on my hair. She waved her hand and said, 'I like your curls.' I could tell from her posture that Leny was a real lady: she sat up very straight with her chin held regally high. Then I met Ida, who was sitting in a wheelchair at the head of the table, her arms folded. She gave me a friendly nod. I noticed right away that both housemates were wearing colour, which I like.

One particular encounter left a deep impression on me and I often think back on it. A chic-looking woman in a wheelchair was sitting at the long dining room table with her head down. Her name was Clara, I was told. She was wearing gold-rimmed glasses and she was draped in elegant clothes studded with pearls. I walked over and kneeled down beside her. 'Good afternoon, ma'am,' I said as I placed my hand on her right knee. With her eyes closed, she produced an incoherent sound. 'I love the shoes you're wearing.' It had no impact, unfortunately;

her eyes remained shut. The lack of reciprocation made me question myself. A silence ensued.

I firmly believe that it's possible to connect with anyone, anywhere and anytime, so not long after, I went back to her. I thought it was important to discover what my housemates thought about me coming here, and I preferred to find out first-hand. This time, I pressed a little harder on her knee and whispered in her ear that we were going to be housemates. Now I did get a reaction. She opened her eyes, which began to twinkle, and sat up straight. In an instant, she changed from a sick old lady into a proud and strong woman. I continued in a gentle voice: 'You're more than welcome to come and have coffee with me.' The invitation had a visible effect on her. It was wonderful to see. Her eyebrow went up in an endearing way and her face came to life. 'Lovely! You can come and visit me too.' It was such a tender moment. I had to choke back a tear. I'd only just arrived and I was already connecting with people.

This belied the general view that people with dementia lack initiative (known as 'apathy' in the medical world) and confirmed to me that my plan was worthwhile. This was very promising. I suggested that we celebrate my impending move by having a cup of coffee together, upon which she added: 'And cake.' And cake. Goes without saying, Clara.

A few weeks later, I was introduced to the nursing

home staff and my housemates' families. Although they expressed enthusiasm and asked genuinely interested questions, I also detected a note of surprise in some voices. Why would a twenty-one-year-old want to live in a nursing home? You'd expect adults to ask that when a curious, curly-headed youngster walks in, but I always had my answer ready: 'I want to experience life in a nursing home so that in the future I can take better care of people with dementia.'

Given my background in nursing, I was asked whether I'd also be helping out as a carer, but I stressed that I'd only be a resident here. I continue to separate these roles because otherwise I could never be a real housemate to my fellow residents. And that's what I've set out to do. I feel it's the only way I can come close to the experience of someone whose dementia forces them to live in a nursing home.

As a carer, I can confidently say that the caregivers' perspective tends to dominate the care for people with dementia. A case in point is the weekly multidisciplinary meeting that brings a whole range of different stakeholders together. They talk *about* the residents' ups and downs, but never actually *with* the residents. That's beyond me. How can you claim that someone is unhappy without actually asking that person? How can you maintain that someone is often depressed without listening closely to her traumatic war stories? Just talking *about* others can never be a good foundation for decision making. Never.

In the run-up to the move, I told those close to me that I was going to live in a nursing home. The initial responses, like 'How awful!' and 'Why would you want to do that?', were followed by lots of questions. It may sound strange, but I'm thankful for those strong reactions because the questions got me thinking. What is it that makes us view the nursing home as something horrible or out of the ordinary? And how come we prefer not to discuss life with dementia? Sticking our heads in the sand is quite naïve because anyone looking to the future knows that we'll all have to contend with dementia in some shape or form. If we want to manage this well as a society, we need to drastically overhaul our approach. But how, exactly? I intended to find out.

With a strange feeling of melancholy, which occasionally made way for excitement, I put the last of my things in the removal van. Like my mother, I'm a bit of a hoarder when it comes to vintage items in the broadest sense of the word, so I had to do some rigorous downsizing. Luckily, I could store the rest of my belongings in my parents' house, a huge farmhouse in the province of Brabant. I got into the passenger seat of the removal van and nodded at Dad. 'See you soon!' I yelled as the van drove away. I was on the verge of swapping my rural home for a nursing home in Utrecht, one of the biggest cities in the Netherlands. Suddenly, the fact that I still had my parents and could always go back to them felt like the greatest luxury imaginable.

As the fields and country lanes passed by, I dreamt of the ways in which my experiences would lead to new insights in care. What would the terms I'd learnt in training – 'self-management', 'autonomy', 'quality of life' – come to mean in my role as a resident? How would I deal with death when I saw the residents not as patients but as housemates? One thing was certain: unlike for my new roomies, the nursing home wasn't my final destination in life. That thought added a whole new dimension to my move.

The sight of the Amsterdam–Rhine Canal really brought it home to me. *Holy shit, it's actually happening*, I thought to myself as the lorry drove into the grounds of the nursing home. *I'll be living in a secure unit. What am I getting into?* But I quickly pulled myself together and thought about the new people I'd be getting to know in a way that had never been possible before.

We parked near the gate, close to my room, and began to unload. Once inside, I spotted a greetings card, with kind words and squiggles that were intended as such. The reality of my housemates captured on a piece of paper. Next to the card was a welcome box, a kind of new baby box, except for the final stages of life. I really appreciated that, as I didn't want to be treated any differently from my housemates. I genuinely appreciated the container for dentures, the urinal, the packs of incontinence products, the protein drink and the bar of chocolate. My new life was about to begin!

The first steps

'Welcome, we're glad to have you with us,' I hear when I open the bathroom door in the corridor.

A bit startled and still a little sleep drunk, I look into the eyes of the night nurse. She has a kind and gentle expression and a voice you wouldn't mind waking up to every morning.

'Did you sleep well?' she resumes.

'Yes . . . not too bad,' I say.

Before I have a chance to compliment her on this warm reception, I hear her next door: 'Good morning, Tineke dear, are you awake? By the looks of it, it's going to be a lovely day, so why don't we put something pretty on today?'

With a smile on my face, I walk back to my room, where the sun is creating a beautiful light show, as if it too wants to greet me on this first day in my new home.

I do a round of the various residences. All is quiet and serene, even the radio and television are off, which is rare in a nursing home. In the corridor outside Residence no. 3, I bump into a housemate, Eugenie. She's dressed in just a shirt and is holding a bra in her hands. When I walk towards her, she looks up.

'Are you lost too?' she asks.

'Yes, I'm still getting my bearings. I'm glad I bumped into you.'

'Yes, I agree.'

I make my way to the seating area in the corridor and Eugenie sits down next to me. I tell her I was given a very warm welcome by the night nurse and that I'm pleased to be here.

'Good, me too,' is the reply.

Then suddenly, the morning shift comes in to lay the table. 'Yay, breakfast!' I exclaim. People who know me won't be surprised by my reaction: I'm always hungry.

With a plate piled high with bread I sit down at the large table in the living area, where, at first, my only company consists of jars of jam and peanut butter. After a while, the door opens. A housemate walks in with a care assistant, happily chatting about the latest news on the ward. The woman is very well turned out and her hair is set in pretty waves. The carer seems to be enjoying her job, she's smiley and full of beans.

'Why don't you sit over there?' she tells my housemate.

'Tineke,' the housemate replies when I introduce

myself. She gives me a firm handshake and a wink, and there's no doubt about it: we click straightaway.

That's confirmed a little later when we plonk ourselves down on the sofa to digest our breakfast. 'The hairdresser did the same yesterday. I never get to . . .' Tineke is lost in thought. 'Oh well, never mind . . . I live here and I'm not a quarrelsome person and I don't always want to put my foot down, but they're giving me a hard time.'

I wonder what exactly is bothering her so much, but she rattles on and on.

'People are free to think they're more important, I don't care. As long as they give me a chance to live my own life, but that's just not on the cards in here. I don't want everything in my life to be managed by other people, that's not what they're here for. They're here to help people.'

Something has happened, that much is clear. And when you're this worked up about it first thing in the morning, it must bother you a lot.

'Don't expect me to just sit around all day. I'm aware it makes me a bit stroppy. But if I get to offload it on you, I'll feel much better,' she says, looking at me for approval.

'Any time, Tineke,' I say, as I take her hand and notice that she's slowly regaining her composure.

Sitting next to me is a strong and lovely woman who's

confiding her troubles in me after only one morning in the same home. Remarkable. And to be made to face the facts on the first day of my new life confirms to me that it was a good idea to move in here. Tineke clearly wants to exercise control over her life and is able to identify when she feels it's being taken away from her. I wonder if she can express herself in this way to the carers – my gut feeling says no. Self-management for people living with dementia is a hot topic in nursing home care, but I'm more and more doubtful as to whether it is in fact possible within the current approach to care. Not according to Tineke, anyway, and I'm very curious to see how my own views on the matter will change during my stay here.

Another housemate comes in. She makes a beeline for the sofa and parks her walking frame in the corner. Then she gives me a friendly wave and sits down. I walk over with the chocolates I bought yesterday as a conversation starter and ask if she'd like one. She doesn't have to be asked twice and she unabashedly plunges her hand in the box. I've seen her before and introduce myself: 'I'm Teun, and I've just moved in here.'

Showing no sign of surprise, she reacts: 'Leny. Leny de Planque.'

The chocolate appears to be a good way to make contact, so I walk back to Tineke. She carefully reaches for one. 'Oh, I've got two,' she exclaims. I laugh with recognition. Whenever I have a biscuit tin in front of me, I always grab the biscuits that just so happen to be stuck together.

My housemate Ida enters and practically jumps out of her wheelchair at the sight of chocolate. She's so keen that before I can stop her, she's already crammed her mouth full. 'I'm glad you like them,' I tease her, which earns me a blissful gaze in return.

As I put the last chocolate into my mouth and take a good look at my housemates, I hear to my left: 'These dentures on the sofa here, whose are they?'

Of course, I think to myself, with a huge grin on my face, *dentures on the sofa. That's life.*

The afternoon goes by and at five-thirty on the dot, it's dinner time. In what looks like a veritable procession, my housemates and I make our way to the table, where the inescapable jar of apple sauce has just been put out. The assistant on the evening shift, a nice, easy-going lady, asks if someone can get it open. She's specifically after a strong man, but in this female-dominated world the options are limited: Lambert and I are the only men present. Lambert Kramer has a roguish look about him and lives in the room opposite mine. His first attempt to open the jar comes to nothing. Then he takes a knife and raps on the lid. Three dents later the jar still isn't open, so he decides to hand it to me. 'Here, you have a go, lad.'

And guess what? First time lucky! Remarkable, because for someone with my physique it's rare to win a physical showdown. 'Brains versus . . .' I begin, waiting for a reaction from one the housemates at the table.

Tineke laughs and shouts, '. . . brawn!' and she continues with a big dose of self-deprecation: 'I certainly don't have the brains today because I spent all day looking for my phone.' Tineke's disarming sincerity enables her to talk about the unpleasant aspects of her dementia and it can be a survival mechanism when your world is getting smaller and smaller. I feel a connection with Tineke, as if I'm already friends with her.

The meal over, I want to go outside. There's an exit but it's locked. My first outing on my own is thwarted by a keypad on the wall, which has buttons worn with frequent use. While I try to remember the code, my eye is caught by a piece of paper stuck to the door. Reading the text sends shivers down my spine: RESIDENTS ARE NOT ALLOWED OUT WITHOUT PERMISSION

Imagine: you feel like you're a well-functioning individual and then you come across this sign. What are you to make of that? Wouldn't that be extremely distressing and undermine your self-esteem? I think this one line speaks volumes about the balance of power in the care sector.

The access code is not the year we're in, so I walk back to the lounge, still stumped by the sign on the door.

When I have the correct code, I try again, successfully this time. A few more doors follow, but luckily they all open automatically.

I'm outside. Bliss. I'm greeted by the humming of cars, the wind and other sounds of everyday life. I quickly put in my earbuds to listen to some music and hop on my bike to enjoy the sunshine and the people in the street. A breeze wafts a bit of cool air in my face. The ultimate freedom, I think to myself, as I cross the canal and cycle into Utrecht's old city centre. At that very moment, I hear 'I Want to Break Free', a track by Queen. Pure coincidence, of course, a random choice by my 'Discover Weekly' Spotify playlist, but it doesn't feel that way today. No, today it feels like everything is going to plan.

Back at the home, I get talking to Lambert, my neighbour across the hall. He has come to have a look at my room, clutching his phone. 'It's getting there,' he says with a note of sarcasm, running his hand through what little hair he has left. 'You get very bad internet here, it's a real bummer.' The problem, according to him, is that the residents' network doesn't reach the end of the corridor. Unfortunately, I haven't been given the Wi-Fi code yet, so I can't check whether the problem is with the network or with his phone.

Good digital accessibility in nursing homes is an interesting challenge for the future because as the modern world is becoming increasingly digitised, so too is the care sector, and that includes secure units. More and more people with dementia have smartphones and want access to the internet so they can stay in touch with friends and family. That's incredibly important, seeing as their relationships with others change so much when they move into a nursing home. But unrestricted access to an entire digital world can bring difficulties, of course – such as violations of privacy, phishing or excessive social media use. In Lambert's case, however, the digitisation process is clearly still in its infancy; the fumbling with his mobile suggests he's still getting to grips with 'that thing'.

Lambert is a lot more familiar with the objects he spots on the wall, as I'm hanging up my vintage album covers. His frustration with the poor signal evaporates in an instant and he starts telling me about the artists he sees.

The music stories and the emotions they evoke bring us to what it's like to live in a nursing home. Lambert doesn't mince his words: 'Shit.' We both fall silent. 'It's boring and it's nothing like my previous life. I used to have my own printing company, but now I'm confined to a little room in here.'

We look at each other. Although Lambert had seemed pretty content at first sight, that image is completely shattered by what I see and hear now. There's no joy in his eyes and I'm deeply saddened by that. Looking for a glimmer of hope that might cheer him up a bit, I suggest we go and visit 'his' printing company sometime.

'Oh, are we allowed out again?' he asks with a sudden twinkle in his eyes. That throws me for a moment because without permission from his legal guardian, unfortunately, we can't do a thing. I tell him I'm going to do my best, but I can't promise anything. It's painful, but the culture of the nursing home can be a far cry from what people with dementia actually want. As far as I'm concerned, exercising such strict control over basic needs is at odds with the theme that has epitomised my first day here: self-management.

I ask Lambert whether he has a wife. He chokes up. 'Yes,' he replies, and I can tell how much he misses her. His anguished tone chokes me up as well. For a split second, I wonder if being in this environment is good for me. I see a great sadness in Lambert and I hope I can maintain the courage of my convictions with so much suffering around me.

Nonetheless, moving here feels like the right decision. Day-to-day life with its myriad emotions and the culture within the nursing home fascinates me, and besides the sadness, I also see plenty of beauty. There's laughter and even dancing when a carer puts on music and holds out a hand to Leny. In the soft evening light they dance around the living room together and I watch my housemate shake her hips. She's so full of life, it's as if I'm looking at a young woman dancing in a night club, right here in the middle of the nursing home lounge. Right here . . . in my new home.

II

BETWEEN HOPE AND FEAR

Life after death

'Are you afraid of dying, Mum?' I ask as I throw my first week's washing into the machine. I find that in nursing homes, the laundry is done on such a big scale that sometimes things are washed too hot or they're never returned, so I'm playing it safe by taking it all back to the mothership.

'I'm . . . No, not of dying. Growing older I find a lot harder. We're all going to die, son, so you might as well be pragmatic about it, and when the time comes, I hope it will be quick.'

Typical: my mother is good-looking, eccentric and middle-aged (sorry, Mum, but it's true), and she'd like to remain that kind of woman until her last breath. At the same time, she can be extremely sensible when it comes to the big things in life – a kind of hippie farmer.

'I love how you cut it down to size. Death is a frequent visitor to the nursing home, so maybe I should look at it the same way.' I open a beer and say: 'Cheers, Mum, to life,' not knowing that within a week, death will stroll into my home.

Two days later, I'm at my usual place at the table, next to the elegant Clara, ready for one of the highlights of the day: dinner. Before my move, I'd been harbouring ambitions of becoming a vegetarian, but after a week at the nursing home, it's clear that now isn't the right time. Like most evenings, we're having a classic Dutch meal of boiled potatoes, vegetables and a piece of meat. Clara's got something else in front of her, practically in her face, in fact, since her head is hanging down. Almost grazing her beautiful wavy grey hair is a small bottle of nutritional supplement, a banana-flavoured drink with extra protein. She doesn't touch it and neither the care assistant nor I are able to get through to her. She appears to be in a deep sleep. When she doesn't consume anything during the next few meal or snack times, alarm bells start ringing for me. *This doesn't bode well*, I think to myself, as I remove her bib. If this continues, death will be inevitable.

For the next two days, I don't see her at breakfast. Does that mean the time has come? I only just got here and I'm already losing a housemate. If she's as poorly as I think she is, they've probably started palliative sedation to keep her comfortable while she's dying. My suspicions are confirmed when I see the doctor and the intern walk towards her room.

Partly out of curiosity, I decide to head back to my digs, and when I pass by Clara's I notice that her door is open. From the corner of my eye, I see her lying in bed. By the looks of it, she's still alive – you can always tell from someone's face, especially when you've seen a dead person before. The doctor and the intern are standing by her side looking at each other. It's still not clear to me what exactly is going on. It's an experience that's completely new to me. In my role as a care assistant, I'd simply ask how she's doing but that feels inappropriate to me now. I made the conscious decision to be a resident, and to avoid any conflict of interest or other awkward situations, I don't want to step out of that role. The last thing I want is to create the impression that I'm keeping tabs on the care assistants like some sort of spy.

It hasn't escaped Lambert's attention that I've gone back to my room. He regularly pops in for a chat, and so he does now. I ask him if he's heard how Clara is doing. Lambert raises his eyebrows. 'I assume she's alive, otherwise we'd have heard about it, right?'

That makes a lot of sense, so I decide to throw myself into unpacking the rest of my removal boxes, which have been sitting in my room for a while now.

Over the following days, I learn little about Clara's

condition, until I bump into her family in the lounge. Have they come to say goodbye? No, they've come to collect her things. Collect her things? While my housemate Lambert was interested to know how Clara was doing, just as I was, she passed on and was taken away by the funeral director without anybody knowing. My elegant neighbour is dead, the first resident I had *real* contact with, and we haven't even had a chance to say goodbye. 'I can't believe this is happening,' I say out loud in the living room. 'Surely this isn't ethical?'

When residents are deprived of something as big and fundamental as news of a death and saying goodbye to the deceased – because apparently it's not deemed to be important to people living with dementia – then what other life experiences are they excluded from? Perhaps it just didn't occur to the care assistants, but it's a thought that haunts me and scares me. It's a reality that's impossible to explain to the housemates I have to share the news with.

The weird thing about my new home is that I'm forever tossed between happiness and sadness. Just a few days later, I'm officially allowed to call myself a nurse. Right before the start of the online graduation ceremony, I decide to quickly introduce myself to my newest housemate, Elly, who has moved into Lambert's room. Lambert has gone back home, to his wife. It turns out that he was living here temporarily to give his spouse a brief respite from care. He was overjoyed when he stepped out the door, a privilege given to very few, and I was so pleased for him because I'd seen his eyes grow more vacant by the day. Good for him. Let's hope Elly is a nice replacement.

I can tell from the sounds coming from the room that her children are here. Wearing my smart suit and with two pairs of shoes in my hands, I appear in the doorway – in my socks, that is.

'Good afternoon,' I say.

Elly looks up from her comfy armchair. 'Hey,' she reacts enthusiastically.

'I've come to introduce myself; we're housemates. I'm the neighbour across the hall.'

She looks surprised and we shake hands.

'I can tell you love fashion,' I say. 'You look so smart. And now that we're on the subject: which shoes do you think go best with my suit?'

Elly bursts out laughing and thinks for a moment. 'Those ones,' she says wholeheartedly, pointing to my grey winklepickers with yellow heels.

With those shoes on my feet and the other pair in my hands, I walk back to my room. The graduation is about to begin. Or rather: the laptop is open. Luckily, I'm not attending the ceremony on my own, despite the many coronavirus measures: Muriëlle and Tineke are here too. Muriëlle is honoured to share this special moment, she says, but she seems even more thrilled when she learns of my sexuality: 'There aren't any gays in my family, although I would have liked that. And that's the truth.' The tone has been set.

Meanwhile, my fellow students appear on the screen. I notice glasses of wine and decorations in the background and everybody is well turned out. This hasn't escaped Muriëlle's notice either: 'I like to see a gent in a suit instead of a pair of jeans.'

I'm sitting between the two ladies, poised to release the confetti, while Muriëlle and Tineke are both holding a glass of white wine. *My day couldn't be any better*, I think to myself, as the official part of the ceremony kicks off: the oath in which I solemnly promise to practise my profession faithfully.

Then the wine is swapped for balloons because we're fast approaching the moment when my name is announced. 'I can tell,' Tineke says when I confide that I'm a bit nervous. When my name is called out, the confetti pops and Muriëlle and Tineke hold up the balloons in celebration.

'Boom!' Muriëlle laughs and Tineke joins in.

'I wouldn't have missed this for the world,' Muriëlle says.

The room is strewn with confetti and our hair is full of it too. When I carefully pick the bits of paper out of Tineke's updo, she becomes a bit emotional. 'I never thought I'd get to experience another graduation ceremony at my age.'

I couldn't wish for nicer words because it was for Tineke, my other housemates and everybody else with dementia that I completed this degree. Getting to share this celebratory occasion with them feels truly special.

After the ceremony, Muriëlle goes back to her own room, but it's not long before she returns with Teunie, who also lives in Residence no. 1. I guess she can't do without me for too long. Muriëlle starts talking about her family. 'I don't intend to meet my maker until I've held my granddaughter in my arms,' she says about Melanie, the latest addition to the family. She likes to talk about her background and childhood. 'Nobody's had the upbringing I've had. I'm a little rich girl.' Born into the Curaçao gentry, she's incredibly proud of her heritage. 'I had a lovely childhood. On Sundays, we used to go to the *baai*, what you call the beach here. And then we'd all cook together, family, friends and acquaintances. Nobody was expected to pay or bring anything. My father took care of everybody. I mean, you can't tell someone without money to chip in, can you? My father could afford it because he worked for Shell, and so he'd foot the bill.'

Muriëlle takes after her mother in terms of appearance, I think, but she has the perfect comeback to that observation. 'I may not look like a Caribbean, but

I make up for it with my heart and temperament.' She sits up straight and proud, like true royalty. 'Eventually we moved to the Netherlands. I was fifteen at the time. My father thought this was a better place to study, and he was right because you're sitting next to a bona fide professor.' She won't tell us what she specialised in. 'It sounds too boastful, so I'm not going to tell you. I don't talk about it because I just want to be myself.'

As she tells us about her past, I'm awed by her eloquence and the strong expressions on her face. Such vibrance and energy. Unfortunately, they quickly fade when I ask about the present: 'What do you make of life at the nursing home?'

She's quiet for a moment. 'I wasn't expecting that question. Let me think . . . I came here because I could no longer look after myself. I would have preferred to stay in my own home but I didn't have the necessary support. So when you're thrown in at the deep end here, you have to adapt. I think it's neither good nor bad in here. And you're responsible for making your own fun because that's not something money can buy.'

This reaction requires further explanation. I ask her how you make your own fun, as I wouldn't mind doing that myself.

'By adapting, and I'm really good at that,' Muriëlle says. 'And every evening I have a special drink. One part custard, two parts Advocaat.' She laughs. 'Believe me, it's delicious, Teun. And they buy it especially for me. So the Advocaat you got me wasn't quite the special treat you thought it was.'

We have a good laugh about the failed surprise. The story about the egg liqueur makes a lot of sense, but I do have some questions about the adaptation bit. Do we residents retain our identity when we adapt to the culture within the nursing home, or are we expected to become completely different people?

'Yes, please,' is the enthusiastic response when I ask Muriëlle if she wants to take the bottle of Advocaat with her. 'You bought the good stuff.' The look on her face suggests that she's pretty pleased with it after all.

'You're quite a character,' I say.

'I've been told that since the day I was born, and I won't change,' she replies proudly, after which she disappears down the corridor with the yellow bottle in the basket on her walker.

After dinner, we all go our own way, at our own pace. For many, that means the sofa in front of the telly, but not for me as I have a lot of reading to do for my new course.

I've been in my room for several hours when, around ten, I hear a gentle knocking. I open the door and see Tineke. 'Do you mind if I come in?' she asks. She's looking a bit worried and tired, and she's more hunched over than usual.

To be honest, I'm shattered because it's been an intense day, what with the graduation ceremony and everything, but I let her in anyway.

Tineke tells me that she wanted to phone Dorien, a close friend. 'Then I was told: "There's no need, it's all been taken care of." About two or three minutes in, I may have said something that then escalated and will come back to haunt me. I feel awful, like I'm on the scrap heap.' Although I can't quite follow her, it's clear that she's had an unpleasant experience. 'Things are happening behind my back. As in, it's all done and dusted, and I'm expected to put up with it.' She swallows. 'And then I had a think about what I feel about living here because I do have a good life. I reckon I might stay here after all.'

Tineke will have to decide whether she wants to stay here permanently. Her court order expires soon and from then on, she'll be living here voluntarily. 'I thought to myself, I need to go and have a word with you because I can't make up my mind. I start stammering, I start . . . I forget things. I don't know what to do.' A silence ensues. 'I'm afraid I can't go back.'

I ask her where she would like to go. 'To the house where we live. And I'm not talking about my old home.' Tineke gently rubs her thumb and index finger together, which I recognise as a sign of stress. 'They just went ahead and arranged it, and I didn't realise. I'd been waiting for one of the ladies, because there was something . . . Oh well, I'm not quite sure. I'm a bit out of sorts. I can't explain it very well.' I ask Tineke what she's afraid of. 'The thing is . . . The room I was in was suddenly not my room anymore. And I was taken to another room. I'm really rattled,' she says sobbing.

'I know, dear Tineke,' I reply. 'It's a lot to take in. Shall I walk you to the room that has the photo of your dog?' I deliberately put it this way because her room doesn't always feel like her room, but when I mention her pooch it'll feel like a safe haven to her.

After I've walked Tineke to her room, I plonk down on my bed in my smart suit. Whoa, what a day! It felt like a kind of turbo-charged blender with a mix of emotions swirling around inside. A day full of happiness from my old world and moments of joy in my new one, but above all an unforgettable day. And before I know it, I go out like a light with the lights on.

I still don't feel completely rested the next morning and I struggle to get out of the shower. Someone tries the doorknob twice within the space of a minute.

'Teun is taking a shower,' I hear the care assistant say in Elly's room.

'Oh, it's busy,' Leny says.

My head being so foggy, I forgot my towel, so I wrap myself in my bathrobe instead. With soaking wet hair and steamed-up specs, I appear in the doorway to the

47

lounge. 'The bathroom is all yours, Leny,' I tell my housemate to her great joy.

I go to my room because I have quite a few articles to read for my course, but I'm finding it hard to concentrate. It feels as if my head is completely blank. My new world is taking a lot out of me and I can't really pretend otherwise. When Elly walks into my room, I push my textbooks aside. She asks me how I'm doing. After a moment's hesitation, I decide to be upfront: 'It's all a bit overwhelming, El.'

'I can imagine,' is Elly's sympathetic response. 'But you're doing really well, honestly . . .'

'Thank you,' I say without looking at her, because I'm afraid I might burst into tears.

'There, there, lad.' She puts her hand on my shoulder. 'Just be you and everything will be all right.'

The big why

This book may come as a shock to someone who's never been in a nursing home, but perhaps the same is true for anyone who has or who works in one. I think very few people would willingly swap their house for a small room like this. I say *very* few because now that I've given my digs a bit of a fun retro makeover, the reality is sinking in. I live in a nursing home! The thought sends my heart racing and I'm finding it hard to breathe. I know this environment like no other, so why this uneasiness? Even though I'm in a secure unit, I'm allowed to come and go as I please.

Then it slowly dawns on me: I feel cut off from the big, buzzing outside world I love so much. It's so eerily quiet in my room and the view so barren that I feel like a real resident. And while that was exactly what I wanted, I never thought it would hit me in this way. 'Okay, Teun, pull yourself together,' I whisper and press the button of the espresso machine I brought with me, because foresight is everything.

Over the next few days, the shock that comes with my new status as a resident proves to be a real eye-opener. It's good to be shocked, I think, because it makes you ask yourself why. And that's an important question if you want to change things, because by figuring out exactly why you're feeling rotten, you may be able to avoid or minimise the sensation in future. Taking the 'Big Why' on board, I suddenly see my new home as an arena full of questions. Why make a nursing home look like an institution? Why make the corridors so sterile? And why expect everybody to live according to the same schedule? In short: why does my new home look the way it does and why do we continue to do things the way we've 'always' done them?

The architecture of many nursing homes most closely resembles a stack of DUPLO blocks. Everything is straight and angular, which demoralises you before you've even entered. But why is that? I'd say it's probably to achieve the most efficient layout, as this design is clearly not conducive to a cosy atmosphere.

Unfortunately, my new home is no exception. Just off Utrecht's busy ring road, you'll find a large car park with a big fence around it and plonked right next to it is an even larger building. It's made of light-coloured bricks, alternated here and there by a horizontal line of grey, a typical institutional style. Now, you won't hear me say that all nursing homes ought to be designed by Rem Koolhaas. No, I'm just asking: why? Why should a nursing home, which aims to be a domestic residence for many, put people off? Surely its exterior can and should be different?

I'm no architect, far from it, but I think you can create a warm and homely atmosphere by introducing life in and around a building. This can be done with attractive construction materials, greenery or even a splash of colour, much as you'd do at home. A friendly exterior makes the whole place so much more inviting. Nobody gets a kick out of walking into an impersonal institution, whether they have to live there or when visiting a loved one or relative.

The second point is location. As we all know, the golden rule of property is 'location, location, location'. That's to say: location is everything. It goes without saying that a house bordering Vondelpark in Amsterdam is more sought after than a house less than a kilometre away by the ring road in Nieuw-West. How come this golden rule tends to be ignored in the construction of nursing homes? The answer is simple: money. The price per square metre in a prime location is unaffordable. It's not that we should build a nursing home on Dam Square, but I do wonder why there doesn't seem to be any attention to the setting of facilities. You'd think that for people who spend all day inside and who are only occasionally allowed out, an inspiring locale is priceless. Who wants to stare at a blank wall or a paved courtyard with a metal gate all day? If you can't go anywhere, you'd kill for a few lovely trees, a glimpse of the horizon or an interesting urban scene, wouldn't you?

Does that mean we should raze all existing nursing homes to the ground? No, I'm not saying that either. The best way forward would be to see how their settings can be improved, and especially how they can be embedded into the surrounding area. Remove the tall fences that give people the impression that these are secure facilities, places where outsiders aren't welcome. Make sure that locals can walk past residents' windows on their way to the supermarket or school. Install a children's playground in the courtyard, a football pitch for young people, a coffee shop for hipsters and older folk alike, the kind where you can smoke for all I care. Link the nursing home with the rest of the neighbourhood because only then will local residents realise that this big building on their doorstep is an actual home for people who like to raise a hand in greeting and who smile when they see children walk past. And only then will nursing home residents feel that they're still part of a community. Out of sight, out of mind; so let's stop hiding people and bring them out into the open.

Inside, the unit where I live has the familiar layout of a large family home: a living room with a kitchen where fresh meals are prepared every day, two shared bathrooms with toilets and a private bedroom for each resident. For a long time, it was customary in the Netherlands for multiple residents to share a room, but in recent years there's been a transition to separate accommodation. This is in line with Western culture, in which privacy has become much more of a priority. You may well ask whether this trend is always beneficial because there may be times when sharing could offer residents the sense of safety and security they so crave. Perhaps the answer lies in the watchword *du jour*: tailor-made care.

As I mentioned, I like a bright, colourful room, so I don't waste any time asking the manager if I'm allowed to replace my heavy brown floral curtains. 'Replace your *curtains*?' It's clear that no one's ever asked this before, so the counter question isn't long in coming: 'Why?'

'Well,' I reply, 'much as I like retro, this is too much of a good thing. And perhaps . . .' – I choose my words carefully, so as not to antagonise anyone this early on – 'they are also a bit too . . . institutional?'

She can't give me an answer there and then, but luckily the facilities manager gets in touch soon after: it's allowed. I already see myself at the furniture village, but before I get a chance to actually go, I receive a follow-up message: 'A number of conditions apply: you must consider fire safety and the fabric must be ordered from a particular supplier.' There go my colourful curtains.

I contact the preferred supplier for a quote for the most cheerful print I can find: a yellowy-orange waffle texture. Two weeks later, I receive a quote for a whopping 1,200 euros. I know curtains are expensive, but 1,200 for barely four square metres? It's crystal clear to me that the supplier's monopoly not only results in long waiting times but also in inflated prices. That same day, I send a friendly email back to say that my student loan doesn't permit this kind of spending, but thank you anyway. Sincerely, Teun Toebes, Residence no. 2, Room 3. I understand that as an organisation, you need to comply with the latest health and safety regulations, but at what price, I wonder. This kind of imposed uniformity comes at the expense of a cosy atmosphere and people's control over their own lives.

The more I look around, the more I realise that the issue of health and safety goes much further than the curtains that first brought it to my attention.

The house rules

Nearly every house has rules, and a nursing home is no different – except that it has a very specific set of rules. From the very first home where I worked to the one I'm living in now, I've always identified a common denominator: everything is designed with safety in mind. Why? What is the reason why safety governs all aspects of life in a nursing home? And perhaps more importantly: what are the implications of this?

Nursing homes are known – perhaps even notorious – for their long, white hallways with handrails on the walls. At first glance, you might think you're walking along a hospital corridor, not least because of the sterile colours and furnishings. The rails are there for a good reason: you really want your residents to be as active as possible, so if they have mobility issues and the rails help them walk, then great. And if that's no longer an option, the rail is an excellent aid for propelling wheelchairs forwards.

So let me be clear: I'm most definitely in favour of these kinds of health and safety measures because nothing would be easier than knocking a quest for better care by saying: 'Teun doesn't care about residents' safety.' I'd hope that people know me better than that by now. Even so, while writing about sensitive issues like this, I always feel the resistance of the care sector flowing through my pen and this tends to make me a bit defensive. But 'why?' is the question you need to ask if you really love the people who live here and you genuinely want them to lead the happiest lives possible. Every minute of every day at the nursing home, I feel that safety considerations have a stranglehold over life. It makes me and my housemates feel that we're prisoners, unable to be ourselves – and all that in the final stage of life (for my housemates, anyway).

Nursing home care in the Netherlands may be among the best in the world, but that's not to say there's no room for improvement. Sometimes I get the impression that we've gone too far in our efforts to care *for* people and we've lost sight of how to best care *about* them. I feel very sad to see nursing home care so far removed from normal life. Often it's just little things, but it's the everyday experiences that make the difference between a house and a home. For instance, why don't we have mood lighting in the lounge? Even with half our current lighting, the place would still be brighter than the average home and we'd be able to see both our feet and potential obstacles. And why do we have to wait for the perfect outdoor conditions before the doors are thrown open and we're allowed out for some fresh air? We like to feel the sun and wind in our face as much as the next person. 'A little bit of rain won't kill us,' I can hear Tineke say on the sofa in the lounge.

Why does all the food have to comply with strict factory-grade safety standards? Care assistants aren't stupid; they're not going to serve up spoilt pork chops. If unsafe food is such a big risk, I'd like to know how many people in this country die of it in their own homes. And why aren't we allowed to keep pets when we all know they give such joy? Why does everything have to be so sterile and so anti-allergenic that my housemates are forced to talk to robot dogs? Why all these changes when they managed just fine before? Just because they were diagnosed with dementia?

It's not as if I only notice these things because I'm young; my housemates weren't born yesterday. When Leny comes over for coffee with Tineke, she's pleasantly surprised: 'Look at the size of that palm, Teun.'

'He's got all kinds of things,' Tineke adds.

Leny notices this sign of life immediately and it's no wonder, because unlike other areas in the nursing home, my room has real plants. Even though there are plenty of non-toxic varieties, at some point it was decided, on health and safety grounds, to install only artificial plants. And straight away that gets me thinking: why? As if people with dementia spend all day eating plants. The only time I've seen a fellow resident with a piece of plant in her mouth it was a fake one with wire sticking out of it, so you tell me which is more dangerous . . .

If you ask me, this preoccupation with health and safety gets in the way of normal life. It's a serious restriction on the freedom of people with dementia, and by extension, on that of everybody connected to them, such as family and carers. Good care calls for seeing things from another person's perspective – in this case, people living with dementia. Like you and me, these are individuals with needs, and like you and me, a small moment of joy can mean a lot to them. A trip to the supermarket, having a nice apple by the canal or a spontaneous cup of tea in their room. My housemates take great pleasure in those things and yet they're the exceptions that prove the rule – or rather, the endless string of rules.

The way I see it, we ought to aspire to nursing home care that's based not on the safety but on the happiness of residents – with all the risks that this entails. The feeling of being alive should always take precedence over 'what if'. This may sound hard, but then so is life in a nursing home. Not so much for myself because, however annoying this feeling of being locked up may be, I know

I can leave whenever I want. But that doesn't apply to my housemates Tineke and Muriëlle, who feel exactly the same. For this reason alone, I owe it to them to write this book. In some respects, prisoners serving custodial sentences are better off than my housemates. People here can go days or weeks without outdoor access, but this would be unthinkable for regular prisoners. In fact, it's laid down in law that an inmate should be allowed to spend at least one hour a day in the open air with the necessary supervision.[7] Can a politician please explain to me why the most vulnerable in our society have fewer rights than convicted criminals? It's unacceptable. It's further proof, if any were needed, of the harsh reality of people living with dementia and shows how we value them as a society.

All it takes is a peek outside your room to see the huge distinctions made between people in ways that would be unthinkable beyond these walls. 'The bathroom's along the corridor, behind the first door on the right,' residents are told. Family and other visitors are directed elsewhere: 'You'll find the toilet halfway down the corridor on the left.' While carers have their own separate lavatory with a key. Residents have asked me repeatedly about this system. 'Do they think we're dirty, Teun?' Muriëlle wants to know.

Because I don't want to bite the hand that feeds me and be disloyal to the residential home that has opened its doors to me, I just say, 'I suspect a lot of people think our loo is a bit scary, Muriëlle, because it doesn't really look like the one they have at home, except for the actual toilet bowl.'

'I don't blame them,' she says, 'because it's a terrible place to relieve yourself.'

If carers really want to get to know their residents, it's important to strive for equality and implement it in all areas of the nursing home system. I'd like everybody to get a sense of what it's like to share a bathroom in which you're greeted by the stench of bags full of incontinence materials wafting out of trolleys that are literally three feet away. Disgusting? Absolutely, but it's the reality in nursing homes. I truly believe that if everybody, including carers and management, went to the same toilet, those pongy containers would be consigned to history in no time. Let's face it: nobody should have to be surrounded by human faeces.

To be honest, I must admit that during my placement and later work experience, I've been guilty of the same behaviour, 'because this is how things are done'. I'd toss the incontinence materials into the trolley and shut the door behind me only to go and do a number two in a lavatory that smelt of roses. It's so easy for a young carer, fresh out of school and with the best intentions, to get sucked into the system without ever asking why things are done the way they are. It's not as if I don't have olfactory organs or I didn't know that making distinctions between people can lead to a feeling of exclusion, but in training, the question of 'why are things done like that?' simply never arose.

During my four-year nursing course, only one half-day was dedicated to dementia, whereas sooner or later we'll all be confronted with it. It's incomprehensible to think that the training of healthcare professionals is playing catch-up to such trends in public health. By the same token, there was never any talk of humanising care and the ways in which we might be able to translate this ideal into reality. You'd think no healthcare curriculum would be complete without this kind of human-centred approach. But, given this absence, I'm really only qualified to care *for* rather than *about* people, something I feel all the more acutely with every word I write. If the human dimension is overlooked in training, how are you supposed to change anything in the field, when all the staff were taught the same approach? You can't really blame them for taking issue with anyone who has a different view. It's no wonder that a young nursing home resident like me, who's asking difficult questions, is seen as a pain in the neck.

I honestly mean it when I say to all the highly valued care assistants in the home where I live: I understand that I don't always make things easy for you. I understand that you find me an annoying know-it-all at times, but I can't help it. I can't see and feel where the rub is without getting people to talk about it, because if there's anyone I believe in, it's you guys. And I mean this from the bottom of my heart. I want to make our future more fun, because changing the way we approach people with dementia isn't more work, it's simply a question of seeing things differently . . . Once you realise that, it's out with the old routine and drudgery and in with greater job satisfaction. I hereby promise you that I'll give my all to try to break the ingrained patterns of dementia care, with its emphasis on red tape and health and safety regulations, as they chip away at the happiness of the people who ought to be our main concern: the residents living with dementia and the carers carrying out their vocation. It's not until we see changes in this area that a nursing home can become a nursing *home*.

III

SAFETY FIRST

Reality check

'Hello. Hello-oh . . .?'
I jolt awake, look around in confusion, grab my specs from under my pillow, jump out of bed and, before I know it, I'm standing in the middle of the corridor in my underpants. Shit, I forgot that I'm in my new home! Then I hear it again, the sound of someone in distress. 'Hello?!' It's coming from the room diagonally across mine. It can only be Tineke, I think to myself, and I walk in. She's trembling with fear, clutching the wash basin, unsteady on her legs. I can tell from the look in her eyes that she's extremely distraught.

'Tineke, it's me, Teun . . . Your neighbour from across the hallway,' I say softly.

'Ahhh . . .' Her voice sounds a bit calmer already.

I take her hand and start stroking it softly. 'It's all right, Tineke. I'm here and I'm here for you.'

'H-huh . . .?' she stammers, staring at me with huge, questioning eyes. 'Where am I?'

'You're in your room, dear Tineke, and everything's fine. We both live here.'

A deep sigh of relief follows and then she gives my hand a firm squeeze. 'Oh, thank goodness, boy . . .' But she's clearly still grappling with something. 'My father was deported from Leidseplein, and all I could do was stand and watch. I was only a little girl. The Germans took him . . .' The panic seems to have given way to a profound sense of disbelief that I haven't seen in her over the past few weeks.

'The war is over, you're safe here in Utrecht, with me. I know what you're going through.'

A bewildered look is followed soon after by a relaxed yawn. 'We're both in our pyjamas. Are you off to bed too?'

Two days earlier, Tineke had told me that most of her family were deported during the Second World War. 'Gassed, all of them . . . The Germans never intended for any of them to come back.' These dreadful events in her early years had a devastating effect on the long life that followed. She's traumatised and has difficulty trusting people. If, on top of all that, you suffer from dementia too, you'd hope that at the very least, you're granted a gentle end-of-life and you get to put all that sorrow behind you. Unfortunately, the opposite is true: for Tineke, sometimes the loss of her father is more vivid than ever. There are times when she can no longer distinguish reality from the memories she's reliving, so she's thrown back into her trauma. It's something you wouldn't wish on anyone, least of all on Tineke.

She lies down in bed and when I notice that my touch has a relaxing effect, I keep tenderly stroking her hand until, thirty minutes later, she's fast asleep again. I plant a kiss on her hand – 'See you tomorrow, Tien' – rub my eyes and see on her old clock that it's half past three in the morning. Good, I can go back to bed for a bit before the first of my housemates appear at the breakfast table.

This moment in the dead of night is one I'll never forget, not only because I lay staring at the suspended ceiling in my room for hours afterwards, but because this is the first time I feel that I'm not just a visitor but an integral part of this remarkable world.

Although these poignant moments have a great impact on me, more often than not I feel as though I live in a hall of residence full of mature students or, as I jokingly called it at a friend's party: 'House VSOP', which stands for Very Superior Old People. The designation normally refers to the age and quality of cognac, with P meaning pale. The nickname sounded funny to me but, on a more serious note, I thought it was a suitable moniker for my unit and my housemates because they could do with some positivity to compensate for the stigma that comes with dementia.

THE HOUSEMATES

My friends at the aforementioned party weren't exactly complimentary about my living situation: 'You're completely bonkers for wanting to live among the old dears.' 'What's the point in living in a place where people forget who you are from one day to the next?' 'Please shoot me before they stick me in an institution like that. No straitjacket or shit on the wall for me.' And so it went on for a while . . . Many of my friends and acquaintances have absolutely no idea what a secure unit looks like or what living with dementia really means. Often, it's only the extreme cases that are plastered over the media and, because so few people are familiar with nursing home care, these scare stories are never offset by more realistic depictions.

Much of the public perception is completely wrong: dementia doesn't make you insane and the era when people were routinely strapped into straitjackets is long gone. However, it's true that you may start to forget things, lose track of the time of day and perhaps your character will change. I'd say that there's most definitely a point in spending time with people who are becoming forgetful or confused because they'll always need human contact and friendship – those are the very reasons I decided to move in here.

One of the very few stereotypes that's accurate is that eventually you can forget how to use cutlery or how to go to the bathroom. And when you don't remember how to do those things, maybe you no longer understand what excrement is and what you're supposed to do with it. 'Is that funny?' I asked my friends. It was dead quiet in the room. 'You'd be lucky to have a friend, relative or carer who doesn't laugh at you or put you to bed in your soiled pants, but who's kind, gives you a wash, cleans your room and gets you out into the world in fresh clothes again.'

And sure, when you read this, perhaps you think you'd still rather be dead than end up in such a situation. But that's easy for you to say. The thing is, you don't get to this state overnight, if ever, because in my experience, these manifestations of dementia are the exception rather than the rule. Even at the most advanced stage, it turns out, that people with dementia and their loved ones don't necessarily want to pull the plug, so please don't go around saying that life with dementia isn't worth living because that can be incredibly hurtful. The fact remains: whatever you think or say, eventually you'll be confronted with dementia, either directly or indirectly. Dementia knows no gender, colour or age, so swap your scorning, joking and judging for looking, listening and asking questions. You actually have a one in five chance of developing dementia.[8] Figures like that force us to consider the possibility of life with dementia before it happens. My advice: start thinking about it now, whatever your age. How would you like to be cared for? At this point, you still get to have a say; later, when you're ill, you won't.

While these kinds of big questions do come up quite frequently as part of my new life with my housemates, I also worry about the little, everyday things, such as my new shower ritual. I still feel a bit weird about making my way to the bathroom in my bathrobe, in front of the care assistants more than my housemates. I'm pretty comfortable in my twenty-one-year-old skin and when I look in the mirror I'm not unhappy at all. Vain? A little bit, yes, although I certainly don't claim to be God's gift to man. I think I've struck a good balance, with my luscious head of curls making up for my small stature. At the same time, I'm not averse to fashion, so in his turtleneck, black designer shoes and oversized retro specs, this brand new nursing home resident walks the corridors looking very hip indeed. I also see myself as fairly masculine, although my housemates seemed less sure about that at first, as I found out when I walked past the ladies sitting on the sofa. 'She has the most beautiful curls,' Leny said to her neighbour. 'Yes, such a sweet woman,' Eugenie added. See what I mean . . .?

Before that stroll to the bathroom, I've often been up and about for several hours. I've always been an early birdcomma and that hasn't changed since I moved here. I'm also a workaholic and never happier than when I have a busy schedule, because otherwise I feel as though

I'm wasting my time. As someone born and bred in the countryside, I love the outdoors. I've recently taken up running along the canal at sunrise. The sensation of the wind on my face is wonderful. After I get back and tap in the entrance code to my unit, I have a quick look to see if anyone's awake and up for a chat. If not, I disappear into my room to check my emails with a nice coffee from my own espresso machine. Why my delight in this, you ask? One, because the nursing home coffee tastes not unlike the canal I just ran along; second, because it's a small moment of happiness when this form of housing doesn't give you much space for yourself. Besides, the espresso machine can mask the somewhat pungent smell of the incontinence material out in the corridor, but let's not go there.

Every morning, I work at my antique wooden table next to the sofa and opposite the bed. On opening my laptop, I usually find some fifty emails in my inbox because while I may be a resident here, I also have the 'ordinary' life of a twenty-one-year-old. Okay . . . ordinary may not be the right word, but there are some similarities. Alongside my Care Ethics and Policy degree, I'm the founder of Article 25 Foundation, a hobby that's grown into a full-time voluntary job. The foundation seeks to enhance the lives of people with dementia by giving them as many happy moments as possible. These can include silent discos in nursing homes with family and friends, as well as trips to favourite holiday destinations, restaurants and former homes or workplaces. We also take people with dementia to visit schools to raise awareness. By introducing youngsters to dementia at an early age, we're hoping to nip the prevailing negative perceptions in the bud. Those with dementia do the talking – we don't talk *about* them.

I'm also busy spreading my message and talking about my mission on social media because my generation and the one below it will inherit a world in which dementia is an integral part of everyday life. In twenty years' time, the number of people living with dementia will have doubled and those figures will only increase further. The so-called 'dementia tsunami' predicted by scientists is going to be a major problem if we continue on our current path. I have tens of thousands of followers on social media, all interested in learning more about my experiences at the nursing home, so I'd say there's a very real need for information among the young. But making dementia sexy enough for it to become a hot topic is a challenge, of course. It remains a distant proposition for many young people, and I totally get that. To be fair, it's far more normal to *not* think about these issues. But can you accept 'normal' as the norm when you want to change the world . . .? I don't think so.

My housemates hail from a time before the internet, and some even grew up without a television or a telephone. (They're the real golden oldies.) So how cool is it that I, a young guy born with a smartphone glued to his hand, can help them discover a whole new world and show them the best TikTok and Instagram posts? Don't worry, I'm not going to create accounts for them under the name Angry Cat or exploit them like some kind of momager would her children. No, from time to time I do a fun video with them – but only with their permission, of course. And before you hurl angry questions at me, their legal representative is okay with it as well. I involve the other residents in both my online and offline life, and they love it! Well, why wouldn't they? Photos have always been popular, even back in the days of black-and-white and pre digital editing. So I often find myself laughing with Ad – the most garrulous person in our group – at the funny stories posted by entrepreneur and influencer Bas-Smit. I'll share journalist and presenter Tim Hofman's latest videos and do TikTok dances with Muriëlle. And let's not forget my swiping on Tinder. It's all perfectly normal, just like I'd do with housemates in student digs, but with the added advantage that here, I'm always the one with the latest scoops and most up-to-date developments. And these new things or new worlds give us a real boost. As Muriëlle keeps telling me, 'If you want to make a video, you know where to find me, okay?!' How cool is that?

It's almost silly to keep saying this, but I hope that

the power of repetition will work its magic here: my housemates genuinely are 'ordinary' people with just one difference – a doctor has diagnosed them with a form of dementia. That diagnosis hasn't robbed them of everything they liked when they were younger, so of course they still enjoy discovering new worlds. Constant stimulation of the mind and the senses is crucial for everyone, even for my housemates with dementia. Or rather, especially for them because when the nursing home environment is all but stimulus-free, the view is stimulus-free and the relationships between residents are stimulus-free because they're all in the same boat, then what on earth are they supposed to be stimulated by?

It sounds so simple and it is, honestly! Ask yourself: what would *I* like to do if I was sat on the sofa all day, or how would *I* like to break the routine? And then have a go. Go on, try. Treat people with dementia as your equals and not as pitiful creatures who've lost their marbles. Truly beautiful, surprising and moving moments do linger in the mind – if not in minute detail then certainly in their overall sentiment. By evening, people with dementia may not remember exactly what happened in their day, but if it was enjoyable or fun, their mood will reflect this. So my suggestion is to create moments that matter – to you as well as to those you share them with.

* * *

It has taken me a while to get used to the mealtimes here. Not because the food isn't good – no, we have freshly cooked meals every day – but because of the strict timetable; I know it's half five, dinner time, when I hear my neighbour's door. Another thing that really surprised me to begin with was the amount of food. You wouldn't know it, looking at my physique, but I eat like a horse. The first time I sat down for a meal and saw my housemates pecking at their food, I was in shock. I sincerely hoped there'd be more sandwiches for me or else I'd waste away. Thankfully, there were plenty.

There are two reasons why people here eat so little. Firstly, metabolism slows with age, so they simply feel less hungry. The second cause is a lack of exercise. My housemates, and many nursing home residents elsewhere, do little or no exercise, which is why they need far less fuel. That's not the end of the world, I hear you think, but it's a worrying development because your muscle mass decreases sharply with little exercise. This leads to poorer mobility, which in turn results in more falls. So before you know it, you're at the table in a wheelchair. This can't be right.

There's a kind of protein bomb that keeps people going when they've lost their appetite: Nutridrink, a brand of medical diet drink. To many of my fellow residents and care assistant colleagues, their use is a no-brainer, but you might wonder how long we should keep administering these beverages – in other words, when has a human life reached its natural 'conclusion'? It's a bold question, but I do want to raise it here. However much I try to stimulate people's happiness in our home, I can see that some really have reached the end of the road. Some have both dementia (an umbrella term for a range of conditions, including Alzheimer's, vascular dementia, frontotemporal dementia and Parkinson's dementia) and quite a few other ailments, and the body seems to be signalling in every way possible that it's had enough. So when is it humane to say, let's stop life-prolonging or life-enhancing treatments? And who makes those decisions? The legal guardian? The doctor? At that stage, the residents themselves no longer have a voice. Is that fair?

I find it incredibly difficult to answer these kinds of questions, not least because the debate tends to evoke such strong reactions. But I'm going to try anyway. I think that in many, and maybe even in most cases, my housemates can indicate whether they're still experiencing any kind of happiness or whether the pain is too limiting for this. Next, their wishes can be talked through with the specialist in geriatric medicine or another doctor before a discussion about the human side of things is had with the family. Pain is never purely physical, even though it tends to be at the centre of decisions like these.

What about those people with dementia who can definitely no longer make their wishes known? Some end up being fed for years, day in day out. Picture yourself in bed all the time, unable to move, with your social functions all but ceased. Your eyes and skin are your only connection to the outside world, yet your brain, heart and lungs just won't give up. There's a good chance that nobody understands what you're going through. Then what? What would *you* want in a situation like that? And what would you advise in someone's else's case? I know what I would do . . .

I'm personally not a big fan of those drinks, but if there's one thing I like for breakfast; it's eggs. Preferably soft-boiled. We were sitting at the table one time when someone asked how long it takes to hard boil an egg. I responded by saying, 'Eight to ten minutes, but soft-boiled is much nicer.' The care assistant on duty quickly disabused me of that idea, making it clear that a soft-boiled egg was definitely *not* an option. As so often, my question was 'Why not?'

'Well . . . for the simple reason that there's a much greater chance of salmonella when the eggs aren't cooked till the yolks are completely hard.'

'Okay, I didn't realise soft-boiled eggs weren't allowed,' I kindly replied, while Tineke looked at me from across the table. She winked at me, sweet as ever, as if to say: 'It's going to be all right, boy.'

THE HOUSEMATES

That day it became apparent to me, yet again, that living in a nursing home is a choice with far-reaching consequences – amongst them, giving up a soft-boiled egg on a Sunday morning. It may be a small thing, but it says a lot about the mindset within the traditional nursing home culture. *And that can't be right*, I thought, and, like a good boy, I took a bite of my overcooked egg.

Perfectly normal

'Teun, we've got a new housemate,' someone says in the corridor and, before I know it, Muriëlle comes shuffling into my room with her walker. If there's anyone who likes a good gossip, it's her. Oh, all right, I admit . . . I'm just as bad.

'A man has moved into our unit,' Muriëlle continues, 'and his name's Piet. Have you heard of him?' I certainly have because Ad, who lives a few doors down, has been friends with him for some time. 'Did you hear what happened to him? You know Roos, that lady who can't walk and who's in a wheelchair? Well, she'd lost her slippers. They turned the whole place upside down but couldn't find them, until her son peeped into Piet's room and guess what he saw on the floor? Exactly, his mother's slippers! In Piet's room!' Muriëlle bursts out laughing. 'As you can imagine, it was all that us ladies could talk about, but Piet wasn't amused. When I was in the bathroom washing my hands, he came in looking irate: "Who do you think you are? You're so full of yourself." "Thanks for nothing," I replied coolly, and I must admit, I chuckled to myself when he stomped off again. Because you know what, Teun? When things are as obvious as that, you don't want to waste any words on them.'

Wow, I thought, how I love this woman. So witty and always good for a wise lesson. Marvellous.

'You need to stand your ground as a woman,' continues Muriëlle, who, like I said, can be quite feisty. 'Because sometimes you get these blokes . . . well, real machos, let's say.'

'So where do I fit in?' I ask as I wash up a bowl for the garlic olives, a favourite snack of hers that we always eat together.

'You're not a bloke, you're a young gentleman.'

My response is a long time coming.

'Did you hear me?' she asks a moment later. 'Blokes are always after the ladies.' Suddenly the penny drops and she remembers that I don't fancy women at all, but men, and within seconds she tries to hook me up with a male assistant. 'What do you make of him?' she asks, not a little curious.

Soon after, I see the door handle turn down. Mrs Meijer walks in with her skirt hitched all the way up.

'Look, there we have Roos,' Muriëlle says.

'Hello Roos,' I say.

'Hello girl,' Roos replies.

'Hello girl? When I had a look in the shower this morning, I was most definitely a boy,' I react with a laugh. 'And my name's Teun.'

The ladies are in stitches.

'Are you serious?' Roos asks. She can't believe it and walks straight over to us, takes a good look at me and then nods, still not entirely convinced. 'Hmm, yes, up close . . .' She turns to the table behind me and starts furiously cleaning the surface. Not that it's dirty, but she's a compulsive cleaner. This type of behaviour can be greatly exacerbated by her dementia. That's when the brakes come off, although Roos herself sees it differently. 'I like things to be spotless,' she says. Less than a minute later, she gets to her feet and shuffles to my cupboard, opens the bread bin, peeks inside, finds it empty, removes my camera from a higher shelf, puts it inside the bread bin and places it on the table. 'There we go, all neat and tidy again.'

I reckon that by now, Roos has picked up and moved everything in my room at least three times, but it's so adorable that I just sit back and enjoy it. 'Great, thank you, Roos,' I say, upon which Muriëlle looks at me as though I'm mad. Nothing in this place escapes her.

'Are you coming this evening?' Roos asks. We're not sure where, but we exclaim in unison: 'Yes, of course.'

'I'd like that,' Roos replies, and off she goes.

Muriëlle is clearly pleased that she's got me to herself again and moves a bit closer. Jealousy is not uncommon in people living with dementia, especially where the attention of that one young resident at the end of the corridor is concerned. 'I think your room is ever so cosy, what with the bookcase dividing your room into two. You can sleep on one side and live on the other. She gesticulates. 'I wish I had a double bed like that. Right now, I sleep in one of those narrow hospital beds, I don't like it one bit.' Though Muriëlle is lucky to have a daughter who washes her bed linen for her, so she gets to choose her own pretty covers. It may seem like a trivial detail, but it can make a world of difference to a room.

For anyone who's never been inside a nursing home, let me give you a brief description of an average room: white.

Is that it? Okay, maybe not, but they contain little more than a kind of hospital bed, a matching bedside cabinet, a wash basin and a mirror, with beige linoleum on the floor. Oh, and white net curtains and those heavy floral curtains I tried to get replaced. All in all, a rather clinical affair. I reckon we ought to look into creating a more homely atmosphere with nice furnishings and colour, like I did in my room. Let residents bring some of their own furniture and add a few colourful accessories – some bright bed linen and a plant and there you have it: a totally different ambience. Oh so simple, but it makes living in a nursing home a lot more enjoyable.

Muriëlle makes her way to Residence no. 1 and, after a short stroll down the corridor, I enter the living room of Residence no. 2.

Leny's already at the table. 'Jeroen, Jeroen,' she says as she looks up at me. She seems confused. 'I'm feeling a bit funny, my mind's gone blank,' she continues. Before I get a chance to respond, she demands to know, 'Is my nose clean?'

Leny often asks me the same questions when I see her. 'Do you like what I'm wearing?' is one. Luckily, I can answer in the affirmative because she always looks impeccable. As she does today. A proper lady in a lovely purple blouse, black trousers and matching loafers. Such repetition could be annoying, but her appearance happens to be extremely important to her. Muriëlle usually looks beautiful too, particularly on special occasions. 'People with dementia are still people,' is how she puts it. 'What they wear or what they look like matters to them, we shouldn't underestimate that.'

It's a fair point and something that, as care assistants, we tend to lose sight of. While the rest of the world is keen to follow the latest trends and project a certain image, we seem to deprive those who've been put behind a four-digit code of this dignity. Tracksuit bottoms, ill-fitting T-shirts and faded sweaters with the laundry service tag still on – just a few items from the latest nursing home collection that illustrate what we think of people with dementia. Here, too, the solution is simple: at the very least, make sure that people who are locked away don't look as if they never have to face anyone again. Enable nursing home residents to look smart, fun, fashionable and well-groomed, and it will have a knock-on effect on their sense of self-worth and their mood. If they choose to walk around in a sweatshirt then that's fine too, but we mustn't allow people to go to seed.

'She always likes it when you do something silly,' Leny says, as she points to our housemate Ida at the head of the table. 'Try sticking out your tongue.' Leny leads by example and, sure enough, Ida responds in the exact same way. It's lovely to see my housemates discover how to connect with one another. I'm learning a lot from them, mainly by watching and listening. As long as I show enough of an interest, they come to me with stories.

When more housemates sit down at the table, I look at the clock. Yup, half twelve, time for lunch.

Leny wants to know when she's going to get something to drink. 'Where's my coffee?' she asks me. The assistant behind me tells me that she doesn't drink coffee, but that information is wasted on Leny right now. In fact, it upsets her because she doesn't feel taken seriously and she makes no bones about it. 'I'd like a cup of coffee,' she insists. And she's right; we ought to take what residents say at face value because that's what they want at that point in time. Where possible, go along with them instead of against them: not only will it make interactions a lot easier, but a lot more fun too.

We're joined by Ad, an incredibly kind man, who addresses my housemate Ida as 'darling' when he helps her with her food. He's very caring of others, me included. 'I'm not allowed to drive anymore, otherwise I'd have dropped you off,' he says when I tell him I've got work to do. Or else he'll offer to read my essays for school. Since moving in, he's become a good friend.

When we've finished our sandwiches and the table is being cleared, I tell Ad that I have an exam later in the week and I'm about to attend my final lecture. 'One last coffee, Ad, and then I really need to get going.'

'What's the exam about?' Ad asks.

I tell him it's about research. He shrugs his shoulders.

'If it were about women, I'd pass,' he jokes.

Tineke bursts out laughing. We're a nice bunch.

Back in my room, I push Tineke and Leny's teacups aside to make way for my laptop, but the peace and quiet is short-lived. I hear Ad out in the corridor: 'Teun, you gotta help me, lad.' He rolls a wheelchair with Elly in it into my room. 'Can I leave her here for a mo?' he asks. 'Gotta go somewhere and otherwise, she'll be on her tod. Laters!' And off he goes.

I call after him with a huge grin on my face: 'Sure, Ad!' By the looks of it, my housemates know who to turn to when they're in a bit of a fix.

Leny wanders in as well. 'Indonesians know how to have endless meetings too, you know,' she says as she looks at my screen. My fellow students think it's funny – another grandma joining them for the lecture. It's in English, but that's no problem for Leny, it turns out. 'It's very enriching, this lecture. My husband, Con de Planque, used to talk about this a lot,' she says while she listens intently. It's cool to think that not only am I becoming a part of their world, but they're becoming a part of mine too. And that's how it should be.

Although I like being with my housemates, every now and then I want to be somewhere else for a bit. Sometimes I feel as though I'm living in a place where time stands still, where every day is the same, with the same routine, the same people and the same view. Sure, sometimes it's rainy, windy or sunny, but that's about it. It can leave me feeling a bit down and restless, and then I really need to break out to see other people. My housemates would love to do so as well; some of them would be only too happy to join me. But I alone am lucky enough to actually get out. When I moved in here, I made it clear that this would be my home, but of course that doesn't mean that I'm *always* here. If that had been the case, I'd have left a long time ago. Is it really that bad? Yes . . . and that has nothing to do with the home itself or the people who work here, but being locked up twenty-four hours a day, seven days a week, in the same place does strange things to a person, to any person. Sometimes it feels like I live from meal to meal until it gets dark and everybody goes to bed. Not that I'm tired at that point because by now, I'm finding it just as easy to doze off on the sofa as my housemates, which doesn't seem quite right when you're twenty-one and in your prime.

That's why I try to take my housemates on as many outings as possible, so they get to feel that they're still valued members of society. Going out to buy crisps and craft beer with Ad for a football match, getting some fresh air with Tineke, taking Muriëlle out for a drive in my old blue wheelchair van . . . ordinary things that inject a bit of fun into life and make you feel alive. Those kinds of activities should be integrated and made the norm within nursing homes. Care assistants, housekeeping staff, management and volunteers all have a role to play in this. When everybody feels responsible for engaging residents in everyday life, residents' lives will change significantly. No more, 'Mrs De Jong, would you like another coffee?' followed by a break with colleagues fifteen minutes later, but instead, 'Mrs De Jong, would you like to join me in making coffee for everybody?'

I repeat: everybody. Sit with the residents and tell them about your day-to-day worries, joys and sorrows. Share them. You'll end up having the most beautiful conversations because . . . well, they're people like us. I can't tell you how often Muriëlle has advised me on love and Tineke has told me to look after myself when I tell her that it's all becoming a bit much for me. When you turn to residents with your issues, they'll come to you too, and that makes the nursing home an extension of your life instead of merely a workplace. Build relationships and make them reciprocal – you won't regret it, I promise.

After a 'break-out evening' with friends in Amsterdam, I arrive at Utrecht station the next day and buy a few bunches of tulips at the flower stall. Everyone's used to me coming and going by now, but I still try to make it into a special moment every time. If anything, it's a way to create extra opportunities for fun together.

Shortly after lunch I arrive in the living room, where I lay the flowers on the table. I can tell by looking at my beaming housemates that they're pleased to have me back, but also that it's Thursday, hairdressing day. Three perfectly coiffed ladies and a spruced-up Ad greet me at the table.

'What have you been up to?' I ask Tineke.

'Not much . . . I missed you,' she replies.

Elly spots the flowers. 'I like flowers,' she says in a soft voice.

'I love flowers, too,' Tineke reacts. 'I used to buy them in Amsterdam. Tulips from Amsterdam.'

The three of us head to the kitchen and put the bunches on the counter. Leny joins us, but she's agitated. 'Are you coming back home with me?' she asks. I tell her I'm staying here because the flowers need cutting. 'Do you want to give us a hand, Leny?' Helping us visibly reduces her agitation, which is good. Unfortunately, there's no vase, so we all go on the hunt for one. Eventually, we find what we're looking for in the other living room, behind a big stack of boxes.

'That's a nice one,' Tineke remarks. 'I think it's a lovely arrangement.'

'I'm glad to hear it,' I reply, as I struggle to get all four bunches into the vase.

When it's done, we place the flowers in the sitting area and decide to sit down. Next to us, the television is blaring even though there's not a soul in sight. As so often, I shout: 'Is anyone watching TV? If not, I'm going to switch it off.' Silence . . . Off it goes! The staff here are quite blasé about television. The thinking is: let's switch the thing on, otherwise it's so quiet, and it gives 'them' something to look at. But if you don't want to watch, it's a major distraction. There's no harm in asking if anyone wants the telly on, but don't switch it on out of habit or sheer boredom.

Just as I press the off button, our most devoted viewer walks into the lounge: Ad. He 'only' watches football, tennis, hockey, speed skating, Formula 1, the Olympics . . . well, pretty much any sport. The rest of the time he's in his room working on his Ministeck.

'Hello guv'nor,' I say.

He doesn't hear me and asks Ida, 'How's grandad?' while rubbing her shoulder. He knows perfectly well that Ida's a woman but he keeps calling her grandad for a laugh. She's asleep, but his gentle touch slowly brings her round. After another pat on the shoulder, he lovingly runs his hand through her hair. 'How are you?'

Ida looks up and slightly raises her left eyebrow, but soon after, her head drops again, and she nods off without a word.

'Hmm, must be tired,' Ad says.

'I think so too. Why don't you join us?' I call to him. And when Ad sits down next to me on the sofa and gives me a playful prod in the ribs – 'Laddie!' – I realise just how remarkable it is to live with these people and to get to call them my friends.

2017

'Teun? Is that you? Do you have a moment?' I hear as I walk past our ward manager's office, which is not actually on the ward itself but in a corridor without an access code.

'Sure, Rita. I'm just going to drop these things in my room, and then I'll be back, okay?' I reply before the sliding doors of our unit close behind me again.

'Gonna get a ticking off, kid?' Ad laughs. He's in the first room, so he hears everything.

'Looks like it, but I'm sure it'll be fine,' I say with a grin.

'You been making trouble?'

'Oh, you know me, Ad, I'm a good boy. I bet she has a question or something. I'll keep you posted.'

As I walk away from Ad's room, past the piano and into the living room, I think about his words. A ticking off, that's exactly what it feels like. It's emblematic of the relationship that I feel exists between residents and staff in a nursing home – a hierarchical one. As a nurse, I never felt it that acutely, but as a resident I do. From the outset, you're made to feel that 'these are the rules and you'd better stick to them'. It stops just short of 'and if you don't, then . . .', but the threat is ever present. Obviously, rules don't have to feel oppressive, and they won't when there's a sense of equality. But that's where the shoe pinches in care for people with dementia because equality is lacking. It's not there in the way we, as care providers, regard the residents, not in the rules we formulate for them and certainly not in our treatment of them.

Locking someone up is by definition not conducive to equality, especially not when the decision was made on the basis of a diagnosis and a care plan and not because a law was broken. The underlying idea is that the residents may be a danger to themselves or society, just like the 'mentally ill' who are detained in high-security psychiatric hospitals. With this 'minor' difference: many of those detainees have committed dreadful crimes that leave us in no doubt that they're a danger both to themselves and to society. That's not exactly true for my housemates.

I've not forgotten that my great aunt put herself at risk when she forgot to take her insulin, but did that give us the right to lock her up? Once Greet was given her medication by the nurse and adjusted to her new day-to-day rhythm (eating, washing, sleeping), she was no longer a danger to herself. And she didn't exactly threaten the neighbours with a pitchfork either. She needed assistance and it ended up depriving her of her freedom, self-determination and voice in society.

But Teun, some people with dementia *do* become aggressive, run off at all hours or do 'crazy' things. Yes, but does that justify us locking them up? People who display that kind of behaviour certainly need our help, but our current approach isn't working at all. I've talked before about the feelings evoked by confinement, and it seems to me that those sensations can exacerbate or even cause aggression or runaway behaviour.

I'm itching to escape after only a few days and I'm allowed to – the only resident in a secure unit who can. When you, a regular resident who's not Teun, feel that urge come on, the reaction will be: 'There now, sit yourself down, it's going to be all right,' and that's it, nothing happens. You'll only want it more because you keep getting the same response: 'No, you're home already, there's no need to go anywhere. You have a room here.' But this place doesn't feel like home; you want to leave. 'God damn it,' you say, and that wise guy assistant with all his lies 'can go stuff himself'. Then, before you know it, all these people with pagers and keys show up, telling you to calm down while they try to shove a spoonful of apple sauce with crushed-up pills down your throat. Panicking now, you try to make yourself heard more forcefully. You're out in the corridor, yelling: 'Let me out!' Not that it makes the slightest bit of difference because within minutes, the medication kicks in and you feel yourself slipping away. The lights go out and not for the last time, because this incident will earn you the label 'aggressive'. Now you're known for exhibiting 'problem behaviour' and if they see no other option, you may just find yourself having antipsychotic medicine and sedatives for breakfast every day. Which is a stopgap measure with long-term consequences because not only will you become less angry, but your empathy will turn to apathy. But hey, it's nice and quiet on the ward again . . .

I'm not in favour of aggression and violence, or against medication, of course not. All I'm saying is that a different approach could well prevent a great deal of violent, fearful or otherwise 'challenging' behaviour. Francien, a good friend and manager of a care farm for people with dementia – where they can help look after the animals – once taught me that it's all about 'the art of seduction', and that has stuck with me. 'When you seduce people into staying, they won't feel the desire to leave.' Most people who want to run away are afraid of being locked up. So if we see to it that this feeling of confinement makes way for a sense of belonging, those locked doors can be flung open.

Should someone feel the urge to leave anyway, then walk with him or her for a while until the anxiety subsides. Within minutes, their desire to leave will give way to a desire to go back to what they know. I've seen this for myself and it works. The same rule applies here: normal treatment equals better care. We all like to see our complaints or fears taken seriously, and that includes people with dementia. We all want to stay somewhere nice, and so do people with dementia. So let's build more nice places where people with dementia can live in freedom. Not in isolation, but as part of our society.

In my pursuit of a better future for people with dementia, I like to lift the institutional veil, as it were, but now that I've been living here a while, I've noticed that the strain is getting to me. I've lost count of the number of times I've burst into tears in my room. I keep feeling that I'm difficult and not wanted here, and that's not because of my housemates. It's like I'm having to walk on eggshells when I want to share with the staff any of my housemates' problems, irritations or observations. It's certainly not always seen as welcome feedback – quite the opposite, in fact. The attitude of some of the care assistants and the way they look at me when I walk into the living room make me feel as powerless as a resident.

That's a shame because most care workers are

wonderful people with big hearts, lots of expertise and empathy for my housemates. But that integrity is overshadowed by the control freakery of a few. 'What's he doing all day?' 'Is he hanging out with her *again*?' 'Where's he going now?' These are the kinds of remarks I hear when I walk around the ward, and they always sound reproachful, so I'm becoming more and more conscious of getting in the care assistants' way. And the terrible thing is that I'm afraid to ask if that's true because I worry about making the situation worse. So I slip into this weird spasm with a half-smile on my face, as if to say, 'I mean well, honestly', and display the same meek behaviour that I see in my housemates. It's shocking to observe it in myself. I see that I'm bending over backwards not to get in anyone's way, and that's ridiculous! I'm sticking my neck out for my housemates, but indirectly also for *everybody* in nursing home care, even if they're not always aware of it. I have the greatest admiration for all the people who work here, but in my role as a resident, I see what else is going on, and I'd like to talk about that from time to time.

There are certain expectations of me as a resident. For example, I'm supposed to join in with organised fun in the evening, even if that doesn't appeal to me at that time of day. I believe you should be free to decide what you like or what you're in the mood for. You should never feel as if you're just being put away or parked somewhere. 'Right, that'll keep them busy for a while,' is something I often hear during activities. Why not turn our living room into a ball pit then? That should keep us entertained. And then I tell myself: don't overreact, Teun, keep an open mind . . .

The fact that a string of such incidents and remarks seems to be stopping me from enjoying my life in this nursing home is something that really bothers me. These are emotions that I'm still struggling to make sense of after several weeks because I was really looking forward to living with my fellow residents and my care worker colleagues. And I'm not the only one who feels like this. My housemates are just as clued up about the way things work here and what people think about them. 'When Nurse Natalie is in, we're not allowed to do anything,' Muriëlle tells me. 'She acts like she's in charge here. I want to stand up to her, but I don't because she'll only redouble her efforts. So I keep a lid on it.' Anecdotes like this break my heart. I have no doubt that the care assistant means well, but it's not enough. The final stage of life in a nursing home ought to be a time when you're free to express yourself and you don't have to be afraid of others, especially when those others are partly paid for with your money. It's unacceptable! It's becoming abundantly clear to me that as a care worker, I don't want to become a cog in the nursing home system because I fear I might get used to the imbalanced relationship between residents and carers. That inequality is at odds with everything that makes care so beautiful to me.

However tough it may feel, it's crucial that we don't shun difficult topics and ethical issues but actively address them. Let me put the cat among the pigeons and start by mentioning a restrictive measure that people would rather not talk about: physical restraints. Or, to put it bluntly, tying people down.

Several years ago, both caregivers and relatives lobbied to end the use of the so-called Swedish belt (which stops somebody from moving independently). It turned out that we could easily do without them and these days, this type of restraint is no longer used in the nursing home. I say 'this type', as several housemates are wearing another – albeit slightly less draconian – variant of it. And while these measures are supposedly in the best interest of the person with dementia and they're taken in consultation with carers and family, restraints always have a direct impact on a person's wellbeing. This is illustrated quite well by Elly on those occasions when she's forced to wear a belt.

As soon as I walk in, I see an empty wheelchair parked in the middle of the living room. A sticker on it says 'RESIDENCE 2'. Elly's sitting in the chair next to it. 'I did it,' she says with a big smile. My eyes are drawn to her socks, which sport a laundry service label, a barcode that specifies who the item belongs to.

'You should have seen it. I helped her into the chair,' Ad tells me with audible relief in his voice.

While Ad has yet to finish his sentence, I check which supply workers are present, because by no means everyone appreciates this 'own initiative'. Fortunately, it's Leonie, who always treats the residents very lovingly. She notices me looking at her, 'What is it, Teun?' We get chatting, and when I tell her that I'm pleased with her enthusiasm, she feels safe enough to tell me what she's seen in the care sector. 'Because I'm an agency worker, I'm usually sent to a unit where I don't know anything about the people, so I have to invest a bit of time first. Unfortunately, I'm rarely given the opportunity to do so because, as a supply worker, I'm also expected to help out on other wards or in other places, even though I'd rather look after the people in the unit.' She describes the balance of power, the strict hierarchy between supply workers and the regular workforce – 'Not just between management and care workers, but also between the carers themselves.'

It's bizarre to see a militaristic mindset so entrenched in a world so far removed from the army. In times of war, I think it would be reassuring and only right for everybody to listen to a commander's orders and act as one, instead of having a discussion during a gun battle. But when it's your job to look after people in a place that's nothing like a battlefield, then what good are such hierarchical structures and corresponding behaviour? When a doctor recommends Tineke takes two paracetamol before bed, you don't have to read it as an order; maybe take it as a recommendation from another team member without putting that individual on a pedestal and inadvertently reinforcing the pecking order. Whether you're one of the housekeeping staff or a cleaner, a spiritual counsellor, physio, ward manager or doctor, in principle, anyone can pitch in when the nurses are busy during a meal. And anyone can strike up a conversation with a resident who's sitting alone or pick up the pieces of a broken coffee cup when there's no cleaner on hand. Isn't that what you do for each other, regardless of job title?

Elly has meanwhile hoisted herself back into the wheelchair with the help of Ad and is already shuffling her way back to her room when a nurse walks by and draws Elly's attention to her belt: 'This restraint stops you from sliding out of your chair, like a seatbelt in a car.'

'Oh, oh, all right then,' Elly sobs quietly.

The footrests are attached to the wheelchair.

'Can she not do without those rests, so she still has some independent mobility?' I ask. I'm never sure whether I can say these kinds of things as a fellow resident, but today my gut feeling tells me I should.

'I don't know,' is the reply, whereupon the rests are folded away again.

'And you're just leaving me here?' Elly asks, sounding crestfallen. She starts crying and seems to be ashamed of the belt. 'I don't like it one bit.' She tries to pull her blouse down to cover it up. 'What's it good for?'

I have no answer for her because I don't know either.

A moment later, she answers her own question. She timidly shows me the black restraint. 'I'd had two falls when the nurse happened to walk by. I asked her what this was. She said: "It's punishment." I asked her: "What for? I look like something . . . "' Elly shrugs. 'Then she said: "When you fall two or three times, you're fitted with one of these."'

I don't want to nod because then I'd validate the punishment. It would undermine my equal relationship with Elly.

There's a long silence.

'Dreadful, dreadful.' Elly breaks, and the floodgates open.

Unable to keep it together either, I take her hand and we have a quiet cry together.

'The thought of anyone seeing this, of admitting to

having to wear this thing. It's not as if it's my fault that I fall. And then I get punished, too.' She's inconsolable . . .

By now, the crying has also caught the carers' attention and Niels comes and sits with us. As far as I'm aware, he's the only member of staff who's addressed by his first name by some of my housemates. Perhaps it's because he's one of the few men here and therefore more memorable, but I think it's mainly because of the sweet way he connects with people. After art school, he decided to come and work in the nursing home and he shows a real, personal interest in my housemates. He takes the time to read the newspaper to Tineke, who's no longer up to it herself, natters with the ladies about important trivia in life and frequently lightens the mood with a good joke. We often find ourselves talking to each other about the dilemmas we grapple with.

Niels tries to comfort Elly as best he can. 'I absolutely disagree with that restraint, but it's not my place to challenge it,' he says.

His words affect me both as a resident *and* as a fellow carer because they speak not only of a feeling of powerlessness, but also of the huge imbalance of power among the staff. We think in terms of positions and titles, and that gets in the way of a more human dimension and approach. It doesn't just undermine the autonomy of care workers, it also stymies the progress of humane care for people with dementia.

That reminds me! 'I was supposed to see Rita, it totally slipped my mind,' I exclaim, and run out of the living room.

At the door, I bump into Ad. 'In a hurry, mate?' he asks. 'Anything I can do?'

'No, thank you, Ad, I forgot my appointment with Rita, that's all . . .'

When I raise my hand to the black box on the wall to enter the code, Ad blurts out: 'You've got that code?'

I'm so taken aback, I start stammering. 'Er . . . yes . . . why?' I'm rooted to the spot, feeling like I've been found out and I'm betraying our equality and friendship by not giving him the key to our world.

'Don't mind me, lad, I'm talking bollocks. See you later.'

Ad closes his door, while that of the unit opens when four digits light up green: 2-0-1-7. Four digits that determine power and powerlessness, four digits that define freedom, four digits that separate our worlds. Four digits . . .

IV

I THINK, THEREFORE I AM

Things were better in the old days

'Wow, look at those kinky trousers you're wearing, very sexy.' The words come from the sofa behind me. I'm in the living room, reading the newspaper, and hear Leny and Tineke titter at their cheeky remark.

'Kinky? Ha ha, this is the latest fashion, you know,' I say as I get up and do a twirl. The trousers are zebra print, which isn't exactly shocking because even in 'their day', it wasn't uncommon for people to wear this kind of pattern.

'The latest,' Tineke says. 'Keep your clothes long enough and they'll come back into fashion, just like all that stuff in your room.' She's referring to my carefully curated retro room.

'I can't argue with you, can I, Tineke?'

On hearing those words, she beams. 'I hear that a lot, yes,' she replies.

Small talk like this makes me happy. It allows us to momentarily forget what's going on and reminds me what good care is all about: letting people feel that they matter. And it's the little things that make the difference, like joking about ultra-trendy trousers, folding laundry together and reminiscing about the old days, or making the ladies blush by telling them about your love life. In other words: simply sharing your experiences with others. This is what most people in the care sector were born to do and what they like best, but, due to the burden of accountability and other non-essential jobs, they don't always get round to it. That's a real shame because it means that carers end up depriving both residents and themselves of a great deal of happiness. The fight between ticking off your tasks and sitting down with people is an unequal one because you're judged on the former. That's quite bizarre in a way, as it means that you're more likely to find yourself out of work if you fail to finish your to-do list, than because you're incapable of really looking after people. It's the world turned upside down, if you ask me.

My colleagues, all hundreds of thousands of them, work in the care sector because they have a big heart and really care about people. So please, please, please, let's make sure they can actually put their heart into their work and do it properly, with time and attention for individuals.

My favourite carer on the ward, Niels, has this gift, and it means that all the residents fight for his attention.

When I wheel Tineke into the living room and she spots him, she can't wipe the smile off her face. 'Hi Niels, nice to see you,' she says right away.

'Hello darling, I'm pleased to see you too.' And he gives her a big hug.

As a permanent member of staff, Niels is always in during the week. He's a great support to me, not least in providing a sympathetic ear whenever I'm struggling. He knows just what to say: 'I'm impressed that you've stuck it out for so long.' It's not that he's disloyal to the nursing home, but he's trying to rekindle the fire and remind me why I'm living here. We both agree on the need for change, because we wouldn't want to grow old in a nursing home like this. So what exactly needs to happen? That's the question we keep asking ourselves. Frankly, we almost always conclude that we want to be treated as normally as possible, in an environment that's as normal as possible. We want to be able to go out, have a cosy, cluttered room and eat leftovers whenever we fancy. No gates, locked doors, sterile floors or temperature-controlled food.

'Will you join us, Elly?' I ask. It's time to eat, lunch is being served. Because Elly can't get to the table on her own in her wheelchair, despite her indomitable spirit, I give her a helping hand.

'You're doing better than you were this morning, aren't you Tineke?' I hear Niels say to my other housemate. He's in the kitchen, watching Tineke make her way to the table.

Ad comes and sits with us as well. As usual, he takes the seat next to Elly, whom he affectionately calls 'El'. Every now and then, Ad asks her how she's doing and you can hear the concern in his voice, as, like the rest of us, he can see that her health is declining fast.

'Would you like a glass of drinking yoghurt or buttermilk?' Niels asks Ad.

He opts for the former.

I ask Leny if she'd like something to drink, whereupon Niels asks me to fetch the protein drink for her.

'I'm glad you're back, because it . . .' Ad can't immediately think of the right word, '. . . it livens things up a bit. Aren't you glad to be back?'

I've had some time away from the home again, though the question isn't directed at me, but at Niels. It's great to see that Niels and my housemates get on so well; it makes for a relaxed atmosphere.

'I certainly am,' Niels replies.

'So am I,' Elly adds, while Leny spreads a thick layer of butter on her bread.

An unfamiliar man walks in. 'Are you the one in charge here?' he asks Niels.

I watch him think. 'Sort of. In here, yes,' he replies.

'We're testing the fire alarm at 2pm. The twelve o'clock test was cancelled, so now it's going to be at two. You don't have to do anything, we just want to check whether the notification is received.'

It turns out that the man recently fitted the call bell system in our unit through which the caregivers can be alerted. Sometimes it's the residents who press the button themselves, but more often than not, the sensor by their bed automatically raises the alarm when they get up. To my mind, this is yet another telling example of the control freakery that epitomises the Dutch nursing home sector.

Leny doesn't talk much when she eats. Now and then she glances at me, and at one point she even winks. She's the first to finish, as usual, and I ask her to pass me the bread.

'Of course, because it's you . . .'

I could easily get it myself, but Leny likes to help. It really lifts her spirits and it often results in a nice chat or a special moment.

'You've got quite an appetite, boy,' she laughs.

When I asked her earlier this week what life is all about for her, her answer was illuminating: 'Helping others.' When she feels she's helping someone, you can see the change in her body language and in her eyes. For a moment, she's no longer the shrunken figure who'll look up briefly when someone walks past before the shutters come down again, but the woman who's travelled half the globe, who's open to any and all ideas, and who's got the best stories. All that by 'just' talking to her about what's important to her, the meaning in life that most people spend a lifetime searching for . . . Helping others.

Meanwhile, everybody else is still eating. 'Would you like a slice of fruit loaf?' Niels asks Tineke.

'I wouldn't say no to that.' It's her standard answer.

'I wouldn't mind one too,' Ad pitches in.

Niels puts the bread on Tineke's plate. She can't see it very well because of her bad eyesight.

'That's perked you right up,' Ad says, laughing.

Ida, at the head of the table, isn't a great fan of solid food, but she loves beverages. She points to the cartons in front of her. She no longer has the words to say what she wants, but she can still point.

'I know, love, as long as it's liquid, you like it,' Niels observes.

Once the sugary substance has been poured into her special drinking cup and it reaches her mouth, the corners of her mouth curl up. Happiness is in the little things.

When 'normal' communication isn't an option anymore, it's vital to understand people's body language. But it takes time to learn to read someone – time, which is so important, but seldom in abundance. Time or priority, which one's the problem? Priorities are set by people who are rarely, if ever, on the ground, who have perhaps never been. The whole point of procedures and systems is efficiency, but the question is whether that concept has a place in care. We don't produce hamburgers. It's our job to provide customised care to people who all respond to and deal with their symptoms differently. How can you hope to apply a single model to them all, especially when that model is designed to ensure that every 'puppet' does what it's supposed to do? It means that people who have been trained to help others end up on a bureaucratic treadmill of control freakery. It looks as if we make more of an effort to document everything in case something happens than to take a more human approach and actually *prevent* accidents from happening. I mean, when all the valuable 'hands-on' staff spend more time in their office than on the ground, what could possibly go wrong?

Meanwhile, Elly has stopped eating. Her eyes are closed and her head hangs down. Her spoon dangles from her left hand. She's fallen asleep. It's happening more and more often, and it makes me very sad. These signs of decline are growing worse and more visible by the day.

While I'm lost in thought, a caregiver walks in. 'It's not the right key; do you have the one for corridor no. 3?' she asks Niels.

'If mine doesn't fit, I don't know which one will. But

there should be someone else around somewhere,' Niels says, while he hands her his key.

She walks off to find out.

'We've got so many keys here,' Niels says with a sigh.

'And now there's the drawers as well. We have to ask a member of staff to open them up for us,' I say. Recently, some of the kitchen drawers have been locked 'for our safety', as if they're expecting my housemates to start rummaging in them and attack someone with a knife and fork. And we're talking here about knives so blunt they barely cut through air.

'It's one of those rules that's observed for three weeks and then quietly dropped again,' Niels replies.

The people that my housemates have the most day-to-day contact with are the caregivers because many friends from their own generation have already passed away, and other acquaintances and relatives rarely visit. Only a handful of my housemates receive daily visitors, so care workers mustn't underestimate the importance of establishing relationships with residents. It takes time and attention, and sometimes a great deal of patience and empathy as well, but it's worth it when you realise that for these people, you may represent the only point of contact with the 'outside world'.

Luckily, we can also bring that outside world into the nursing home and make the lives of people with dementia a bit more pleasant. In our home, for example, there are lots of activities to liven things up a bit. As I said, the compulsory nature of them is a bit of a sticking point for me, but I think you can never have enough going on.

Now that the days are lengthening and the temperatures rising, I feel like going camping. That said, I wonder why people with dementia never go on holiday. After a small-scale survey to gauge interest among my housemates, I take the bold step of asking management whether I'm allowed to take my festival caravan out of storage and park it in the courtyard. 'Because if the mountain won't come to Muhammed, Muhammed will go to the mountain.'

The idea is received with a big smile and, soon after, for the first time in ages, my housemates can spend summer evenings outside a caravan, wine and tropical soundtrack included. It brings about a radical shift in the dynamics, just as it does when I'm on holiday with mates. The new location, the music and the sun make for a rarely seen level of relaxation and merriment. The stories of past holidays become more risqué as the wine gets warmer in the evening sun: Ad's first kiss with his wife, Muriëlle and her conquests. Tineke takes it all in with her familiar big grin. We're only a few metres from our rooms, but it feels like we're in the south of France. Magic!

Once you're in a nursing home, you're in for the

long haul. Visiting places or people is rare. Personally, I love going places, so, one quiet Thursday afternoon, I ask Elly: 'If you had the choice, who would you want to visit?'

Without a moment's hesitation she says: 'My son!'

'Excellent, then we'll go and see your son next week. Leave it with me,' I reply excitedly, at which Elly looks at me with utter disbelief.

All it takes is a single message and, barely a week later, Elly and I are cruising along the motorway in my 'blue banger' on our way to her son, Marcel, and his wife, Petra. 'So wonderful to be outside again, all this greenery ... I can't tell you how much I'm enjoying this,' I hear from the wheelchair in the back of the car.

The reverse parent–child relationship that's developed over recent years is temporarily reversed because this time, she's visiting without her son's help, allowing her to fully embrace her role as a mother instead of a nursing home resident. It's a short-lived return to the old days. I notice that it does something to her because she's behaving differently towards me: suddenly, she morphs into a hyper-critical backseat driver, an attitude that suits her to a T as a former teacher and one that puts me firmly into the pupil role. 'Keep your eyes on the road, now,' she says when I talk to her while driving. 'Go easy on the accelerator.' 'Stop swerving.' And best of all: 'Did you see that car?' Yes, Elly, everything's under control . . .

A little later, I notice in the rearview mirror that Elly is tilting to the right; she's watching the meadows. 'It's all so beautiful, so bright green.'

'Nice, eh, El?' I say, with a big smile on my face.

We approach the exit after barely ten minutes, but the short ride already feels like an epic road trip. 'We need to get some petrol,' I say.

'All right,' Elly responds, but I notice that underneath the blanket her hands are suddenly fidgeting. 'The thing is, I don't have any money on me,' she adds.

I assure her that I have money and that everything will be fine. It's not an uncommon situation. Few ever stop to think that people with dementia in a nursing home never carry money or pay for anything, even though that's something they've done their whole lives. Not having any physical money feeds into the feeling of dependence and isolation from society, which can be easily remedied with a debit card and a wallet with some cash. When I go to the supermarket with Ad, I always say at the checkout: 'It's on me, Ad. You get me an ice cream sometime, okay?' 'Consider it done,' he'll say happily. Don't turn it into a big thing, but at least acknowledge the issue.

As I put petrol in the car, I watch Elly's delighted face through the window. She's spotted some children in another vehicle. Their father is also filling his tank and the kids are pressed up against the glass, pulling silly faces.

'I used to teach little rascals like that,' Elly tells me when I start the engine.

A wide street in a busy neighbourhood brings us to Marcel and Petra's house. The wheelchair ramp is already in place and the couple is standing in front of the window, waving at us. Elly waves back enthusiastically. They come out and immediately capture the moment in a photo. Elly's crying happy tears, overcome with emotions.

'She's looking forward to it,' Marcel observes.

'Careful you don't catch a cold!' is Elly's motherly advice to Petra, who's come out without her coat on.

We go in and Elly's tears of happiness keep coming. 'Such fun,' she says in a trembling voice.

'It's a bit of a change to have you visiting us,' Marcel adds. 'You look well.'

Even though Elly is deteriorating and her legs are growing thinner and thinner, she radiates energy during this visit. 'It's so nice to know where you live,' she explains.

Her words touch a chord with me because they emphasise just how far removed from normal life Elly is. As a mother, you obviously want to know where your child's house is, although it may well slip your mind again. Her son has lived here for over thirty years, but Elly can't remember visiting before. The house meets with her approval. 'You must have worked nonstop.' Elly's humour is back.

'We're having a good old time again,' Petra says.

Elly looks around with interest while Marcel sits next to her, holding her hand. French chansons fill the living room, music that Elly's late husband enjoyed listening to. 'It's really beautiful,' she sobs.

Marcel asks if Elly is pleased to be here. The answer is unequivocal: 'I love it, I . . . Just visiting my son. I'm always thinking: I wonder how he's doing?'

The photo of Elly in the car is sent to the entire family. 'Sjors sends his regards, too,' Petra says. He's Elly's grandson.

Elly looks proud.

'Tears of happiness,' Marcel notes.

'They are,' Elly says.

'You'll get me started too,' Petra says.

They talk about the whole family, so Elly is up to speed on everything. Her eyes are wide open. It's been ages since I've seen her respond to her environment and those around her with such mental clarity. Her health is declining but the impact of this visit is immense. Family strengthens and clearly restores her to the person she is: a strong, funny woman and a proud, radiant mother and grandmother. I'm briefly part of their happiness –

happiness in the purest and most fragile form. It's an experience I'll never forget.

Of course, I'm not going to preach that caregivers should start organising visits like this because that would be absolutely impossible. Many of my followers on social media are under the impression that I get paid to do fun things with people with dementia. If only! In that case, I'd have both the best job in the world and the money to pay my bills. No, everything I do for my foundation is on a voluntary basis because it's fun and important to me. Alongside my degree, I also work a few hours as a nurse, and I obviously get paid for that, so I don't have to borrow even more from the DUO. (For readers who are neither Dutch nor students, DUO stands for *Dienst Uitvoering Onderwijs*, the organisation that's responsible for student loans in the Netherlands.) So who's going to arrange these outings? We are, as a society.

The most likely candidates are, of course, the friends and family of those with dementia, and to them, I'd like to say: HELP! After the nursing home medical staff, you're the ones who have the most say, and that means you're in a position to occasionally colour outside the lines. Tip: try to get the staff on the ward on board with your plan or else you'll come up against a brick wall. Invite your father, mother, brother, sister, grandad, grandma, friend, passing acquaintance or former neighbour to your home. For a cuppa, cake, birthday, dinner, wedding, christening or funeral. Make your loved one part of your life again, if they're not already. Ask if you're allowed to park a caravan near the nursing home for a week and go camping together. Ask if your pets can come and frolic in the garden. Ask if you can have a birthday barbecue in the courtyard. Whatever you do, please involve my dear housemates and the hundreds of thousands of others forced to live with dementia, in normal life. Be difficult and keep trying, and if you can't get it done, send me emails, WhatsApp messages or contact me on Facebook, Instagram or LinkedIn – I mean it – and I'll see what I can do. But I hope it won't be necessary. I hope that all nursing homes in the Netherlands are prepared to sit down with us and look at how we can realise plans like this and even help us initiate them.

Healthcare organisations and staff don't have to arrange everything themselves, but without them, nothing's possible. So here's my appeal to them: HELP! Work towards a more inclusive society by opening your doors, by supporting the ideas of friends and family and by proposing your own solutions when residents or entire wards are at risk of becoming isolated from the wider world. You and you alone have the authority and clout to instigate change within your institutions. Use it to let in a breath of fresh air, to create a more humane care sector – because it's *doable*.

Lastly, there are those who bring in the outside world without doing anything out of the ordinary: the volunteers. To you, the people without a payslip or answerability, I would also like to say: HELP! But not before I've thanked you from the bottom of my heart because you're priceless! Priceless for us as residents, for the care sector and for the families. Without expecting anything in return, you're trying to make the lives of people with dementia a little better, which is truly admirable. The only problem is that we need more heroes like you. So if you're reading this and you're interested in doing something, then sign up to volunteer and come in for a chat. You bring fresh stories and experiences, precisely because you're an outsider, and we need that. Whatever your age, if you've got time and you want to make a difference in the lives of others, drop in!

If my housemates are to be believed, things were better in the old days. 'Back then, we used to help each other out.' 'Back then, family was everything.' 'Back then, older people were listened to.' But I personally don't believe in a better past; I believe in a better future. And I hope you do too.

Silent night

'Teun, you're calling very late.'

As I feel the freezing cold take hold of my hands, I burst into tears. I'm standing somewhere by the side of a cycle lane, my legs trembling, and I've just called Justus, a guy I've known for six months. Our acquaintance has grown into a real friendship. In fact, he's the only one I talk to about the nursing home because I'm concerned that if my mother and my other friends were to realise how I feel, they'd worry day and night.

'Teun . . . are you still there?'

'Yes . . .' I say through the tears.

'Has anything bad happened?'

I let out a deep breath and say: 'I can't go on, I really can't. I have to get out! I grabbed my bike and went for a ride and . . . and . . .'

'Easy now.' Justus's warm, deep voice has an instant soothing effect. 'What do you expect, man? You're twenty-one. Is it any surprise you want to get away from that place from time to time? Don't be so hard on yourself. Your housemates adore you.'

'Yes, but . . .' I begin, frustrated, and look around to see if anyone can hear me. All I see is a swathe of dense ground mist and the diffuse light of the nearest lamppost. 'Sorry, I don't mean to take it out on you in the middle of the night, but I don't feel welcome anymore and I get the impression that the carers really don't like me.'

Justus is quiet; I can hear him think. 'No,' he says calmly, 'I can't imagine they don't like you. Do you know what I think it is? Maybe they're afraid of you.'

Afraid? Of me? That's all I need! As I get back on my bike to furiously pedal away the freezing cold and the anger, Justus says: 'Think about it, Teun, you're a carer who's moved into a nursing home; you have opinions on things that have been done a certain way for donkey's years and then, on top of it, you actually broach all those delicate issues. What did you expect? Did you think they'd be jumping for joy to have you? I'd suspect you were a spy or something. Or, at the very least, a young, cocky know-it-all who's looking over my shoulder and getting in the way.' He's winding me up a bit, which is the best way to get me to put things into perspective. 'Talk about what's bothering you and ask what they make of you, that's bound to take the chill out of the air. Go to bed, Teun. Don't worry and . . . Sleep well!'

I put my frozen phone hand into my woollen coat

pocket. The city lights sparkle in the icy conditions. 'It'll be all right, Teun,' I tell myself out loud, and I cycle into the wintry night, wistful but relieved.

In the days that follow, I go easy on myself. At the same time, I try to gently put my new life lesson into practice and 'openly discuss emotions at work'. I'm surprised at the response. I was expecting to see shocked or even indignant faces, but I notice that the care workers actually welcome the conversations and suddenly show a greater interest in me and my observations. Reaching out to them not only results in a more positive and equal relationship, but it also shows that the divide between residents and staff is not just experienced by the former, but also very acutely by the carers themselves. During our conversations, I keep hearing that they, too, feel powerless, as their roles revolve almost entirely around specific tasks, which leaves little or no room for human contact. 'We have no time to sit down and have a nice chat with people, like you do.' The frustration is evident. 'I'm lucky if I can get through all the work, let alone go for a walk or a trip to the supermarket with a resident!'

The problem of excessive workload is all too familiar to many of my colleagues. It's also something that receives a lot of coverage in the media. In my role as a resident, I've come to understand the effect better than I did as a carer. If you spend all day working your way through a list of tasks, and you never have the time for fun or quiet moments with residents, you're bound to feel that you can't do anything right. Slowly but surely, any enjoyment is sucked out of your job and replaced with stress, and you ultimately end up at home with burnout.

Meanwhile, the fallout from unhealthy workloads is really beginning to show. Not only is absenteeism at an all-time high, but the sector is also facing an acute staff shortage.[9] Put bluntly: care isn't seen as sexy, least of all care for people with dementia. And I understand that because once you've taken away the core of the profession, what's left? When caring for people turns into caring for their physical needs only, then caregivers do little more than keeping those folks alive. Is that really what nursing home care should be about?

Despite their ailments and impairments, nursing home residents want to be seen for who they are and not be reduced to mere patients. So allow carers the time and space to do what they're good at: caring for people – for their physical wellbeing but even more so for their happiness.

We're in that mad run-up to Christmas, but I've realised that in my new home the 'festive' period has an entirely different meaning. There's a bit of tinsel here and there, but for the most part, my housemates seem oblivious to yuletide. It's not surprising when you think that without family, there's not much left of the biggest family get-together of the year. The odd one is lucky enough to be given a wreath to hang in the window, but only a few will actually join their relatives for Christmas dinner. Heartbreaking is the word that springs to mind.

Of course, the big question that many of us grapple with every year is this: when and where do we celebrate? Although I don't have in-laws right now, I'm facing an equally difficult choice, as I've acquired a new family in the form of my housemates. I make a conscious decision to see what the holidays in my new home are like and to spend Christmas Eve with my 'other' family in Brabant.

As with most families, there's food and wine in abundance, so on Christmas Day I arrive at Utrecht Central Station with a serious hangover. On my way to the nursing home, I spot Sjaan, Piet's wife, on her bike on the other side of the junction, and we arrive at our destination at the same time.

'This is my first Christmas on my own,' Sjaan tells me straight off. 'Piet moved here around the start of the new year.'

I ask if she's finding it difficult.

'Yes,' she replies. There's much sadness in her eyes and for a moment, it looks as if it's all becoming too much for her. She's quiet for a few seconds, but then a smile spreads across her face. 'But . . . I'm glad I'm allowed to join you for dinner today.'

Piet is the only one in our unit who still has a spouse. The vast majority of the residents are women and many of them widows, because of the lower average age of death for men. A gap that has actually decreased significantly in recent decades.

We walk to the main entrance together. I'm glad that Sjaan has been invited to attend our Christmas meal as a family member, an exception that should be made a rule as far as I'm concerned. It means neither Piet nor Sjaan is alone, so it's a win-win situation. Once we're through the doors of the secure unit, I'm pleasantly surprised to find everybody in high spirits. We can hear staff laughing, there's music playing and everybody looks lovely. I'm particularly happy to see a waving and visibly improved Elly. She has been so poorly recently that she rarely left her bed, and her daughter has already said goodbye in her head several times.

'So nice to see you again,' I say to Elly, and give her a hug.

'Really nice!' Elly says.

Soon after, we sit down for our meal. The whole thing is incredibly well-organised. The table is beautifully decorated and even has contrasting colours that make it easier for the residents with bad eyesight.

'What do you reckon, do I look nice?' Leny asks, as she runs her hands through her grey hair. She sits down opposite me and gives me a good once-over. 'You're smart too, a real gentleman.' My suit is clearly to her liking.

Meanwhile, Tineke comes and sits next to Leny. She's helped by a carer, who gently ushers her to the chair. 'She's always nice and always sits down beside me,' Leny says, pointing to Tineke.

Like the previous evening at my mother's, there's plenty of food, which is beautifully served by one of the bubbliest assistants on our ward. She's such a role model to me, and not just because she's the same age as me or because I recognise a similar kind of passion for people with dementia in her; I've noticed that she often lets my housemates make their own choices and in doing so gives them back some longed-for autonomy. She's a great asset!

When everyone's stuffed to the gills and we've wiped the chocolate from our lips, Ad suggests we clean the kitchen. He doesn't normally jump at the chance to do this, but today isn't just any day. He proudly coordinates the loading and unloading of the dishwasher and keeps a close eye on everyone. Every fifteen minutes, he yells into my ear, 'Are the plates done yet?' because he obviously wants me to take the dishes out. It's good to see him so energetic.

I'm convinced that everybody has a contribution to make to the nursing home household, but unfortunately for much of the day, my housemates are merely passive onlookers: they just sit and eat and take part in the odd activity. We really need to start doing things together – carers, family members *and* residents. Don't just bring the outside world into the nursing home, but make sure that the everyday things people do at home, such as cooking, making tea and coffee, cleaning windows and doing the laundry, remain a part of residents' lives. It stimulates them and helps create the homely atmosphere that you're after as a residential home. And how cool is it that when a housemate wants to do the dishes, one of the carers can grab a chair, relax and have a chat?

As the day progresses, other staff wander in. After our festive Christmas lunch, the American TV channel TLC is on. My housemates don't seem overly interested, unlike our latest supply worker. Sitting next to me is Elly. She has artfully manoeuvred her wheelchair in between the other seats. But whereas earlier in the day she'd been very upbeat, now I hear the occasional sob. Worried, I ask her what's wrong.

'I'm scared. It's dark and I have to go visit my father.'

Lately, she's been talking more and more about her father. Right now, I understand her thinking only too well. This isn't the first time she's told me that she's scared of the dark, and of course Elly ought to be with her parents at Christmas. She had a Catholic upbringing and Christmas meant a lot to her family.

Using both hands, Elly grabs the restraint around her

waist and says, 'And do you know what's worst? This. *This* is excruciating.' There's a note of aggression in her voice.

The supply worker hears Elly and gives her a sympathetic look. Then she draws the curtains.

Elly takes my hand and starts crying. 'Nurse, I've had it. I've really had it . . . I feel so, so, so trapped.' She's utterly inconsolable, and I feel her unhappiness and frustration pulse through my own body. 'They want to lock me up. I don't know what to do with myself. It's like I'm dead.'

The restraint frustrates me as well. It can be undone with a green button, but this requires a lot more strength than the average elderly person can muster. Elly can't possibly do this by herself, so I lean over and with some effort manage to click it open. It's something that I didn't really want to do as a housemate, but her words hit me so hard that I have no choice. Elly instantly relaxes and rests her head against my shoulder.

The interaction hasn't gone unnoticed. 'They're used to you,' the supply worker says in awe. A well-meant compliment, but the harsh reality is that within a short space of time, I've seen two carers look on helplessly while Elly fought for her freedom. It definitely puts a damper on the cosy Christmas spirit because, let's face it, how is it possible that both the resident herself and the carers in attendance oppose this restrictive belt and yet

Elly has to keep wearing it? I'm aware that sometimes it's the children of the resident who are behind the measure – they insist on it to prevent their mother or father from falling – but that's not what happened in Elly's case. Incidentally, I suspect these family members would react very differently if I were to ask them what they'd want in a similar situation: being stuck in a wheelchair all day or able to walk around freely and risk a fall? I think the answer is obvious because movement is such a fundamental liberty.

Why not let me choose to live, potentially fall and maybe die as a result rather than languish miserably in a wheelchair . . . and then die anyway? Why should a disease, condition or whatever you want to call dementia stop you from taking risks that are an integral part of a healthy life? Why am I allowed to do anything and everything that's bad for me when I'm compos mentis, whatever the consequences, but if I have dementia I don't even have the freedom to walk? I believe that nobody has the right to take those choices away from you. Nobody!

So as not to leave any room for doubt in the future, I hereby want to make it abundantly clear that if I, Teun Toebes, am ever diagnosed with a form of dementia, I want to keep walking. Keep walking till I hit the ground. And when that happens, it's fine, perfectly fine. Because I will have lived till my very last breath . . .

I haven't lost my mind, you know

'This thing gets me places,' says Janna Veenstra as she enters my room on her mobility scooter. 'And I'm the only one on this ward without dementia,' she adds for good measure.

'Ah! Hey Janna!' I splutter, taken aback by her cunning remark. 'Of course I know you don't have dementia. Coffee?'

The main rule in dealing with people with dementia: don't contradict them if you don't have to, go along with the world they describe. This is their reality and by challenging it you'll only confuse them, which can result in stress, panic or anger. So agree with them, even if someone in the secure unit of a nursing home says that he or she doesn't live there.

Because of the stigma associated with dementia, residents are often ashamed to be seen as 'one of them' and will pretend to be still 'of sound mind'. In my view, it makes dementia even more tragic because not only are you helpless in the face of it, but you also have to contend with feeling that the whole world thinks you're crazy.

Unusually, it so happens that Janna's claim is correct because she's here with physical problems, or somatic symptoms, to give them their proper name. She's lived here for ages and is very fond of her room, so when she heard that the ward was to be totally restructured to make way for people with dementia, she was adamant: 'I'm staying put.'

'Do you like to read?' I ask when I see her eyes skim my bookcase.

'Yes, but other things. Not books about ... Alzheimer's,' she reads out loud. She looks at me and carries on in a sarcastic tone: 'Hmm, fun reading matter, just what you'd expect in here.'

Her remark clearly shows how entrenched the stigma of dementia is in society – down to our very own unit. Even in this nursing home, where everybody needs help, including Janna herself, there's evidence of a pecking order. It's shocking to me because, if anything, this place ought to be a safe haven for people with dementia. Yet I can't really blame Janna for thinking along these lines. Normally a very kind and incredibly sweet woman, in front of other 'healthy' people, in this case me, she doesn't want to be seen to belong here. The stigma appears to be so huge that dear Janna momentarily turns into a mean old lady, for fear of what I'd think of her. Isn't that absurd?

It can be extremely tough and confrontational to see people deteriorate and suffer, but what we're seeing are manifestations of the disease, not personal shortcomings. I don't want to focus too much on extreme symptoms because they don't reflect the reality of people with dementia, and to do so would only increase the indelible stigma. Like I said earlier: the smearing of faeces, total oblivion and strange or aggressive behaviour are pretty rare. These symptoms can occur in the later stages of dementia, but six out of seven people with the disease die of other causes before it comes to that.[10] How come it's the extreme cases that shape the public perception of the disease? Is it media coverage or a lack of education and awareness? And, more importantly, how do we get rid of the stigma and make room for a new take on people with dementia and a new way of interacting with them?

To begin with, let's look at how we might normalise dementia, overcome the shame and reticence, and engage people in a proper dialogue. A warm community – think of informal carers, relatives, acquaintances, sports buddies and colleagues – can make such a difference in the lives of people with dementia. These people can all help start a conversation around the subject and explore how they might handle the symptoms in a sympathetic way. Let's face it, if the people around you can't even do this, then how hard will it be for outsiders? So don't run away from it. Please! If you do, you'll not only isolate the person with dementia, but also his or her partner and immediate family, who are probably already shouldering a heavy burden. Talk to one another, including the person with dementia; don't just talk *about* them. Share the difficulties and stresses, but also focus on all the things that are still possible. Have fun together. Life doesn't stop after the diagnosis; on average, someone with dementia will live for another eight years,[11] so make the most of it together.

At the same time, we must ensure that children encounter people living with dementia as early as possible. Doing so will give future generations a different image of these individuals and will also break their social isolation. My housemates would love it if a primary school class came in to bake biscuits. Children's happiness can stimulate those who receive so little other stimulation. So, readers from the education sector: think beyond the petting zoo or the swimming pool and organise a school trip to the grandpas and grandmas and do something fun together. How about inviting them to become reading volunteers in school or why not include a nursing home in the route of a charity walk? Not only will this give children a more realistic picture of dementia, but it will also reduce and hopefully eradicate the fearsome stigma altogether.

But, as so often, the biggest responsibility lies with the government. It's up to them to make dementia inclusive, which may sound like a buzzword, but is in fact an urgent necessity. In twenty years' time, the number of people with dementia will have doubled, in the Netherlands as well as worldwide. It's no longer five minutes to midnight, but five *past*. If the government fails to take action and doesn't prioritise dementia right now, society is bound to become destabilised. With a shortage of suitable accommodation and three-quarters of people with dementia living at home, the repercussions will be felt all through society. While people with dementia will be a common sight by then, the dreadful stigma that currently surrounds the condition could see this huge group reduced to second-class citizens. You don't want them to be completely cut off from the rest of society, languishing at home and putting immense pressure on the community and the healthcare system.

What you *do* want is for dementia to no longer be a dirty word and for us to start seeing people with the condition as an integral part of society, who can participate in our social and working lives for as long as possible and without any shame. Maybe this has you thinking: yeah, nice idea, Teun, but it's not going to happen, is it? To which I say: it's up to you because the state of affairs I just outlined is your future too! Whether you're a prime minister or a secondary school student, rich or poor, one thing is certain: you'll be confronted with dementia. Do you prefer the first or the second scenario?

A few weeks later, I walk into the living room to find Janna again, except not in the state I'd like her to be; she's slumped forward, practically face down in her plate of mashed potato. I go up to her and gently rub her back. 'Hi Janna, how are you doing?'

Slowly, and in a bit of a daze, she sits up. Two hollow eyes look at me. 'Oh, it's you. I didn't see you there,' she says softly.

I put my shopping bags on the floor and sit down in the chair beside her.

'I can't wait for it to end,' Janna says bluntly.

I'm taken aback and ask if I've heard right.

'Yes,' she says with a deep sigh, 'this is no way to live.'

I gulp and we look at each other. 'Would you like to continue this conversation in my room?' I ask.

She doesn't have to think long. 'Let's do that.' She tries to stand up. 'But you'll have to help me out of this chair.' I notice that her first attempt to get up drains nearly all the energy from her emaciated body. I pull the chair back a bit and hold her upper arm. With her last remaining strength, Janna clutches the table, then hoists herself up and into her mobility scooter. 'Right . . . there we are.' There's a note of surprise in her voice.

On our way to my room, I hear the carer ask if Janna has eaten anything. 'A little bit,' is her response.

'Are you coming to my room?' I ask again because Janna is heading in the wrong direction. When she enters my room her driving skills are completely non-existent. In fits and starts, she first drives her mobility scooter into the doorframe and then into my wardrobe. Eventually, she comes to a standstill against my sofa. The enterprising and quick-witted Janna I used to know is gone.

'I don't know what's wrong with me, and none of them really care whether I eat or not. Do you know what I want?' Janna asks me.

I think I know, but don't say it.

'I want it to end,' she continues. 'I'm nearly ninety and look where it's got me. I've had a beautiful life, but not anymore.'

All is quiet for a while; in the distance, I hear the television in the lounge.

'The only person who still cares about me is Ada, my daughter, and I need to keep going for her or she'll be devastated. But to be honest, I've had enough.'

When I ask Janna whether she's afraid of dying,

she doesn't have to think long. Her voice carries such conviction that I practically feel it in my bones: 'No, not at all. Why would you be afraid of that?'

I ask if she'd like a cup of tea.

'Ah, nice . . .' Slowly I'm starting to see the odd glimmer of the lively Janna I'm so used to. 'And let me give you some advice about tea,' she resumes. 'And if you laugh at me, I'll whack you over the head. When you invite people to tea, you shouldn't serve it in such a tall, slender glass because it'll take them ages to drink and they'll never leave.'

'Haha, nice one. I'll remember that,' I reply and feel emboldened to ask further questions about the subject that seems to loom so large in the room. 'Do you ever talk to your daughter about death?'

'Never,' she says firmly, 'because my daughter doesn't want to know. I don't want to cause her any distress because she doesn't deserve that.'

As I take another biscuit, I ask whether she feels lonely much of the time.

'Yes,' she says, and starts talking about Ada again. 'My daughter's really sweet. She visits a couple of times a week, even though she works four days as well, so I can't blame her. But I really miss my husband, he was everything to me . . .' She's clearly putting on a brave face. After a brief pause, she continues. 'We understood each other so well and we had a really good marriage.'

She looks at me with fire in her eyes. 'We were never – I'm sure of it – never, ever unfaithful. Not even emotionally.' A few tears well up, which soon make way for a beaming smile. 'Occasionally, my neighbour would ask if I was worried that he'd cheat on me, but I wasn't because I knew that if he was hungry for it, he'd come to me.' Janna reflects a moment. 'Of course, it's not just about sex, it's about the heart. Sex is important but not the main thing. I'm sorry I wasn't the first to go, but he wouldn't have been able to cope. I really believe that; he loved me so much.'

'But now that you no longer have a husband . . .' I start.

I don't get the chance to finish my sentence. 'Are you mad? Another man, perish the thought! I'd rather be dead.' Janna is gradually coming out of her shell and looks nothing like the woman I saw earlier, lying practically face-down in her plate of mashed potato. 'It's nice, having a candid conversation like this. I never have these kinds of chats. I wouldn't know who with.'

I smile at her and she smiles back.

It's true, we don't have enough deep conversations round here. What strikes me time and again when housemates come to see me is that as soon as the door closes, my room seems to turn into a kind of confessional, a safe haven where nothing is off limits.

'How would you want to die?' I ask.

'I haven't really given it any thought.' She asks if I have.

'I'm not entirely sure yet, but I want to learn more about voluntary euthanasia.'

'That's a good idea. That way, it's up to you, provided you're in your right mind.'

I promptly ask what it means to not be 'in your right mind'.

'It takes away so much,' Janna replies. 'I may have lots of ailments but at least I haven't lost my marbles.' Her answer suggests that she's clinging to this dignity as a kind of last resort, as though losing her mind would be even worse than losing her life.

'I think I'd better head back to my room,' Janna says, and gives me a tender and resigned look.

I accompany her to make sure that she gets there in one piece, and when we reach her room we shake hands.

'Thank you for the pleasant conversation, Janna,' I say.

'You too, dear, I really enjoyed it. But now I'm tired and I'm going to have a nice nap. See you soon.'

A week later, I walk back to her room and write in the book of condolence outside:

Dear Janna, rest in peace. And if you're reunited with Kor, enjoy it to the fullest! My very best, Teun

Normal life

*K*nock, *knock.*
    'Come in!' I practically shout, so it's loud and clear enough to be heard by any housemate. The door opens and in comes my good friend, like he does at least three times a day.

'Hello Ad,' I greet him warmly.

'Hello lad, how are you getting on? Do you need a hand with anything?' It's a question he often asks, as Ad likes nothing better than to go places with me. No, that's a lie, there's one thing he likes even more.

'I certainly do, Ad, because it's Friday afternoon and that can only mean one thing.'

He doesn't have to think twice about this and exclaims, 'A drink, of course!' and reaches for the fridge door in one fluent motion.

'Haha, excellent, that tradition has really taken hold.' I fold my laptop shut.

I liked the idea of introducing Friday afternoon drinks

to the nursing home to lighten the mood, but, even more so, to bring in a ritual from the outside world.

Ad used to work in the energy sector and drinks on a Friday afternoon was a well-established custom in his workplace, just as they are elsewhere in the land. It's no surprise then that he's one of the first housemates to have been granted the honorary title of 'a regular'. As in so many other organisations, the Friday drinks have become a highlight of the week. And that's not just because we love a drink and the snacks that go with it, but also because the group dynamics are turned on their head, as they are in an office or other workplace. It won't get to the point where Elly's dancing on the table or Ad and Muriëlle end up kissing among the pot plants, but it does make the walls and the locked door of the ward suddenly feel like a distant proposition.

'I wouldn't mind a craft beer, Ad. I'll have the one with the pink and yellow label.' I'm chuckling to myself because I know what's coming.

'Er . . . *Mannenliefde*?'

'That's right, Ad, "love between men".'

Now I crack up laughing because he looks absolutely gobsmacked. 'What kind of name is that for a beer? That doesn't seem right, does it? What do you say, Teun?' he asks as he pops the cap off like a seasoned barman.

'Oh yes, Ad, it's all the rage these days. It's made by a brewery in Amsterdam.'

By the looks of it, Ad is completely transfixed by what he's taken out of the fridge. 'A pale ale . . . it's all very peculiar but, then again, that's kind of your style.'

While his dry wit and the facial expressions that go with it often make me laugh, at the same time I melt whenever he puts his lovable spin on things. Ad really is a big softy who wears his heart on his sleeve, someone who may well put his foot in his mouth at times, but who means no harm.

'I'll get my own brand, if you don't mind.' He takes one of the classic brown bottles with the red-and-white label. 'Right, cheers, lad,' he says cheerfully, after which he brings the bottle to his lips and tilts his head back for a big gulp.

As I sit there and admire his 'old routine', I'm surprised that he hasn't said anything yet about the absence of a crucial ingredient in his favourite beverage: alcohol.

'Ah, that's nice. Not as good as it used to be, but still . . .'

There we go. Ad's on an alcohol restriction plan, something his son arranged with the carers and that doesn't sit well with him. Far from it. 'They could've talked to me about; I'm not gaga, am I?'

'I know, Ad, of course you're not gaga,' I say to reassure him.

Under the plan, Ad isn't allowed alcohol during

the week and only two 'real beers' per day over the weekend. An arrangement that's difficult to swallow because it was made without consulting him, something I reckon nobody likes, but least of all Ad. He says he has no idea why the measure was introduced and, as a resident, I didn't want to get involved, so during my first few weeks here I watched how he handled his drink. Obviously, I'm not an addiction specialist, but aside from some lame remarks about the flavour of alcohol-free beer, I've never known him to have an excessive thirst for alcohol. Not even when we'd occasionally loosen the reins a bit in my room, even during the week. (Yup, I'm guilty.) After two or three lagers, I'd usually hear: 'Right, those've gone straight to my head, lad. I'd better be heading home.' He never asked me for more and I never saw him stagger off. That's why I've taken it upon myself, as self-appointed publican, to occasionally provide my best friend with a bit of what he fancies when another prohibition looms. Not because I thumb my nose at those in charge or at the agreements made with his son, but because I want human needs and Ad's happiness to take precedence over these rigid rules and regulations.

I think it's unacceptable that people with dementia are so rarely involved in arrangements. This has to change because right now, we're effectively treating them like children. Is that how we see them? Come on! It's a common analogy – people with dementia become childlike again – but I can assure you that that's nonsense. If my housemates were like children I'd have run off a long time ago. I didn't move into a nursery. I moved into a home where people may forget things or get confused, but at the same time do remember lots of other things. Every day, I have profound conversations about issues like climate change, loneliness, faith, sex, politics and death; I'm given advice on love and help with my studies; and I get to cry on my housemates' shoulders – things I certainly don't do when my young nephews and nieces come to visit.

As the ladies from the unit start to pile into my room, the bowls of crisps are put on the table and Muriëlle brings out the garlic olives, I hear my two male neighbours select a nice beer from the fridge.

'Whoa, this one's pretty strong. See that alcohol content. There it is, seventy-seven.' Ad says.

'Except it says seven point seven, so it's not that bad,' Piet replies, staring fondly at his bottle of beer. 'It's a tasty . . . a tasty number.'

'I like spirits, too,' Ad says. 'I've told my father that I need a bottle of jenever in my room so I can enjoy a drink in my room at the weekend.'

The two men clearly see eye to eye on this. 'Of course, sometimes a nice chaser is just what you want,' Piet agrees.

When Ad starts talking about his Ministeck collection, Piet suddenly gets up to leave. 'Right, it's been fun, Ad, but I'm off.'

Ad is surprised and asks if Piet really needs to go, since he hasn't even touched his beer.

'Yes, I'll only have another one and then another one,' Piet says. 'I need to do some work, you know, round the corner.' Just before he leaves the room, he looks over his shoulder and promises to be back later in the evening.

'Don't forget!' Ad calls out, but probably in vain. Piet slips into wandering mode, which is something he can keep up for hours.

Ad does stick around. He's visibly pleased to be talking to everyone and to have some company in the evening, an evening that's only just started, if you ask him. He nudges me and winks. 'There's only two of us, Teun, the others are all women, so we're in with a chance.'

Just for the record, I remind him that women aren't exactly my target group when it comes to love, but that message doesn't seem to get through. He goes up to Elly and says: 'Fun, isn't it? This, er, happy hour.'

It's moments like these that make me happy and that show how little separates our small society from the big one out there, beyond the green gates – the world we look at and are so close to, physically anyway, but that's so far from us in other respects.

Luckily, these trains of thought are frequently interrupted by some less predictable things. 'These are so well made,' Elly suddenly exclaims, as she studies the crisps.

'That's all done by machine these days,' Ad reacts.

One of the carers decides to pop her head round the door. 'This looks fun,' she says and walks over to Elly. 'I've got a little pill for you.'

'Oh, another one.'

Ad is also given his medication. 'How did you know I was here?' he asks, sounding like he feels caught out.

'Nurses always know everything,' she says with a naughty smile. 'Make the most of it, Ad!' And with that she walks back in the direction of the living room.

Yes! I think to myself. Someone who understands exactly what's going on here and who lets it happen. Because, well, why not?

The morning after this festive conclusion to my hectic exam week, I decide to spend the weekend doing absolutely nothing except chilling with my housemates – because if there's one place that's good for chilling, it's here. I sit down for breakfast in my bathrobe and, shortly after, I plonk myself down on the sofa between Leny and Tineke with a cup of weak filter coffee. 'That was some party, wasn't it, ladies?' Although they both slipped away early yesterday, they're already having a bit of a snooze again.

While I'm keeping half an eye on *Tommy Teleshopping*, I notice the sound of the TV becoming softer and softer in my head until – bam! – I jerk awake to find that I've got coffee all over me. Nodding off is one of my main talents. Like my housemates, I can fall asleep on cue, even though such 'power naps' leave me feeling incredibly groggy, as if my body has entered some kind of hibernation mode. On days when I'm supposed to study, that's not ideal, but on days like this I make no effort whatsoever to fight it.

For me, this is a rare occurrence, but for the ladies on either side of me it's their usual rhythm. If they were to wear a pedometer, the gadget would shut down in shock after twenty-four hours because for them a normal day goes something like this: from bed to table – from table to sofa – from sofa to table – from table to bed or sofa – from bed or sofa to table – from table to sofa – and finally from sofa back to bed. All in all, that's easily some seven relocations of eight steps each, which brings us to a grand total of 56 steps. And that's the sporty ones I'm talking about, because for those with the bad luck of being in a wheelchair, the number is reduced to . . . zero.

If I sound cynical, it's because I *am* cynical. Your whole life you're told to keep moving, that 'exercise is the key to good health', but the weird thing is that I never hear this at the nursing home. How's that possible? How come nobody here is encouraged to move around more, let alone exercise? It's not as if they are all, irrespective of their dementia, in possession of excellent health or a great BMI. The downside of not moving is that it reduces your muscle mass and with it your mobility, so you're more likely to end up in a wheelchair and move even less. It also causes obstipation or, put differently, bowel obstruction. So in addition to declining fitness levels that lead to worsening health and weak muscles that reduce your mobility, you'll find that, like your bowel movements, you aren't going anywhere.

Two hours later, the television is switched off and our slumbers are over. Lunch is ready: tomato soup with bread. The food is fresh and the table looks inviting. As I head over with Leny, Tineke come across the stuffed toy-like robot dog along the way. It barks when it detects motion and Tineke gently rubs its head. 'Dear boy.'

It's extraordinary to see Tineke interact with the dog, but at the same time it makes me feel sad. Why not a real dog, I wonder? My housemates have the time, the garden is big enough and it would also give them a bit of exercise. My guess is that it has to do with hygiene, as the nursing home has health and safety regulations in abundance. As you reach the later stages of life and you're plagued by all kinds of ailments and physical discomforts, you shouldn't be exposed to any additional risk, the thinking goes. However, I suspect that few have died of a dog hair in their food or a bit of cat piss in the corner. Even so, I put it to you: would you rather pet a robot or a real dog later in life? Just asking.

To me personally, this robot dog feels like an impoverishment, like the embodiment of an artificial world. And this trend doesn't end with mechanical pets. Another example is magic tables – devices that project digital butterflies and flowers onto tables. They encourage people to sit down and reach for those images. As a cue for 'physical and social interaction' they're a great idea, but they do require residents to sit at a table. And that's the problem, this endless sitting. Just take people outside to look at real butterflies and flowers and talk to them! If that's no longer an option and the only alternative is to keep everybody sweet with a computer game, then I'm extremely worried that we may have forgotten what care is really about.

Then there's the phenomenon of the door and wall stickers. No, not of your favourite band or animal, but decals that are supposed to trick residents into believing that their mass-produced door has metamorphosed into a castle gate, a rustic French entrance or the ultimate, the ubiquitous bookcase. They are used to transform white walls into green forests. 'It really livens up the corridor,' I often hear. Or, 'It's very lifelike, isn't it?'

My answer is always: 'You think so?' Do you really think that someone making their way down a white corridor full of walkers, wheelchairs and laundry carts suddenly imagines himself in Burgundy when he reaches the 'castle gate'? Does it really bring the forest any closer? I'm not saying this to pan all new ideas that are put forward or because I oppose any form of automation and artificial decoration; I'm saying this because I think we're overshooting the mark when we start investing in solutions like this instead of in people.

As you'll have gathered by now, I'm all for colour and cosiness, but please make it familiar to people, make it real! Real materials, real furniture, real crockery, real plants and what have you. When you live in a world that sometimes seems scary and new, it's especially nice when all the fittings and furnishings look and feel as authentic, warm and ordinary as possible. As if you're at home, say.

So let's not throw out all the old things and furniture overnight and turn the comfy living room into something out of an interior design magazine, complete with 'clean' white-wash laminate flooring and 'trendy' chairs. But we could look to make the nursing home a bit brighter and cosier. Put a few pretty lamps here and there so we can switch off those harsh fluorescent tubes, ask relatives to donate something fun – maybe an old jukebox, a pinball machine, musical instruments, pretty paintings or designer furniture – and create a nice atmosphere together. And do me a favour, will you? Don't let care become a one-size-fits-all solution, because you wouldn't want that at home either.

Human forever
A conclusion

It's a lovely Sunday morning in May, the spring sun is shining full on my face and, as I look at the fresh foliage on the trees through the windows, I hear faintly in the corridor: 'Happy birthday to you, happy birthday to you . . .' Tears trickle down my cheeks. I'm happy to be a year older, but there's a bitter edge to it as well: while I'm in the 'prime' of my life, I'll probably have to say goodbye to several housemates in the coming year. That thought is very upsetting to me. I've grown to love them so much in the past year and some of them have become true friends. My hug with Elly when I emerge from the bathroom in the morning, the deep conversations I have with Tineke and the banter with Ad have become part of my life and I wouldn't miss any of it for the world.

'Teun? I haven't forgotten you, lad,' I hear just outside my door. That can only be one person: my friend Muriëlle. If there's anyone who knows how changeable

155

life can be, it's her. She went from a worldly, privileged life in the Dutch Antilles to life at its most basic in a twelve-metre-square room behind the closed doors of a dementia ward. And she's still so positive! It shows a strength and a resilience that I'm a little jealous of. I can only hope that some of it rubs off on me for when I need it in my own life.

The door opens and Muriëlle softly hums another birthday ditty. 'It's your birthday and I know you're still young, but how old did you say you were today?' she asks as she turns her walker round and sits down on its seat between the handles.

'Twenty-two, Muriëlle, just over a quarter of your age,' I say cheerily, wiping away a tear.

'Gosh, that's a fine age. Promise me you'll make the most of it?'

As the tears well up again, I nod and give her a big hug. 'I promise!'

At that moment, I resolve to take her words as a guiding principle, not just for the rest of the day, but for the rest of my life as well.

'Coffee?' I ask. 'And I have some treats left from yesterday.' I take one of the boxes of the Bossche bollen – Dutch profiteroles – I picked up the day before. We decided to hand them out straightaway because storing all 120 choux buns in the nursing home overnight wasn't an option.

'Oh yes, Teun, did you think I'd forgotten about those? I know when to pop round, haha! I'll have the biggest one. Yum!' This is why I love Muriëlle so much: a young and sharp mind wrapped in a beautiful 'retro exterior'.

When I head over to the living room after this clandestine birthday moment, I find the decorations up over the dining table and, after some prompting by today's carer, I'm even serenaded by my housemates. It's very special to be celebrating life with people who are deemed to have little cause for celebration, people who deserve a beautiful life, but are often deprived of one. Those who I love so much – my housemates, my friends, my new family.

On their behalf, I urge you: help! Help make the future for people with dementia one full of hope, where they're treated with dignity and as equals, in which they're not excluded but fully integrated in society. In short, a future in which people with dementia matter!

Please see a person with dementia as:

An equal person (equality)

Article 25 of the Universal Declaration of Human Rights states that all people have the right to a good standard of living, regardless of age or health. That means that illness must never be allowed to undermine the equality of human beings and that dementia must never be a cause for unfair treatment – ever!

That's why the current unequal legislation must be replaced with something that can guarantee equality and give people with dementia back their self-determination, as those things touch on the very core of our personhood. We have a duty to uphold a person's self-determination for as long as possible. In the event of severe behavioural problems, we must try to manage them without depriving them of their fundamental human rights. Only then can we change the unequal balance of power in care. Only then will the 'patient' become a resident and the carer a guest, because that's how it should be. That is how we increase the likelihood that residents will experience the nursing home as their *home*. They're renting accommodation inclusive of care, so why not treat it as *their* home? If you were helping someone who still lives in their own home, you wouldn't barge in to switch on your music or the TV without asking, so why would you do that in a nursing home? Let's see the nursing home as belonging to the people who live there and make sure they feel at home.

This also means talking and consulting *with* and not *about* the residents. Don't you think you'd still want people to ask you about things, consult you and then take it from there? The desire for control over your own life doesn't go away after you're diagnosed with dementia. When that control has been legally taken from you, 'autonomy' is no more than a hollow marketing phrase in the care provider's brochure. Let's give people with dementia back their voice, so 'autonomy' takes on real meaning and the relationships in the nursing home become more equal and humane. By treating a person with dementia as an equal, we shift the focus from taking care of a patient to caring for a human being.

A person who matters (inclusivity)

Muriëlle once said something that has stuck with me ever since: 'Life here has no purpose, and when you no longer matter, you might as well be dead.' That says it all for me: you've not only lost your voice when you live in a nursing home, but also your role in the world.

Let's make the lives of people with dementia meaningful again. Reintegrate them into society. Throw open the doors of the nursing home so people don't feel confined anymore. It's half the problem solved because being able to leave isn't the same as actually leaving. Do away with the tall fences and hedges around nursing homes and show that there's nothing to hide, that these are places full of people who are beautiful and who matter, and who, like you and me, like to see what the neighbours are up to. Let's build campsites, cafés, restaurants, swimming pools, coffee shops, playgrounds and day care centres on site or close by to foster social interaction with the neighbourhood. Organise a summer barbecue in the garden, ask those who live nearby to give the nursing home a cosy make-over, organise a Christmas social or dinner with the local school, plant flowers together or pop in for a coffee and just chill – whatever you do, stop locking up and locking away. Let's create a sense of community, like I occasionally see in small-scale healthcare organisations.

It's all about vision and implementation, so think small scale and act large scale. By small scale, I simply mean listening to people and creating a comfortable place that makes them feel at home. This can be done anywhere, I'm sure of it. Let residents themselves indicate what they need and work with them to establish a 'normal' warm home where they'd rather stay than leave. Make a *home*!

A person of value (dignity)

Let's treat people with dementia with respect. Help break the stigma by not talking about 'demented' or 'senile' people or dementia 'sufferers', but about persons living with dementia. You wouldn't talk about people with cancer in a denigrating tone, so why would you refer to individuals with dementia as crazy? It's not only incredibly condescending, but it also reinforces the stigma attached to 'those' people.

Reducing people to a particular identity is damaging

to everyone, including persons with dementia. An illness or disorder doesn't make everybody the same, especially not something as complex as dementia, which is an umbrella term for a great many different conditions. If you want to get it exactly right, you should say, 'That's a person living with a form of dementia', but I'll settle for 'person with dementia' to begin with. When you see people as a group, you not only lose sight of everything they represent as individuals, but you also create a distance that makes it easier for you to take decisions that could impact them negatively. 'Those people are ill and best locked away on a closed ward when they become troublesome; it's not as if they'd notice.' Harsh words, but unfortunately not uncommon. But what if one of those people is your mother? I don't think you'd feel the same way. You love your mother and, knowing that she's not crazy and that it would make her incredibly anxious, you wouldn't want her to be locked up.

When you're struggling with a care dilemma, I urge you to think about what you'd want for your mother, father, brother or sister. I'm sure your social and moral compass will point you in the right direction. We will only see change when care becomes personal. You view things differently when you replace a random person with someone you love. Would I leave my brother in a closed ward? Would I let my mother be strapped into a wheelchair all day because she might have a fall? Would I like dad to sit all day?

And of course you can also ask: what would *I* want in that situation? That's the question I've put to myself for the best part of a year in this nursing home and that I continue to ask. And I can tell you, that question works wonders. It radically changes your perspective and helps you to rely a lot more on your social compass. Here's an example: how would I feel if I wanted to go out but wasn't allowed to because a heatwave protocol is in force, even though it's only two degrees warmer than yesterday? Don't we all react differently to high temperatures? Why can't a carer pop out once or twice to check if I'm okay, surely that's not too much to ask? These questions came to me one day when Ad wanted to go outside and I put myself in his shoes. As a care worker, I'd never asked myself these things.

To come back to the stigma: how would I feel if people thought I was crazy? How would I feel if nobody took me seriously? How would I feel if nobody *really* listened to me? Everybody should ask themselves these questions because, as I wrote earlier, you have a one-in-five chance of these scenarios becoming reality for you.[12]

That's a terrifying statistic, but together we can get rid of the stigma. A stigma has no real substance and can be eradicated as easily as it's created. We can do so by sharing information that reflects the truth.

People with dementia are people like you and me, right to the very end. They're people with needs, with feelings, who want to matter to others. People with dementia have a life after their diagnosis, so let's make sure it's as happy as possible by not excluding them but integrating them into society. A dignified existence shouldn't be an option but a guarantee, regardless of age or health.

A person you can connect with (reciprocation)

Reciprocation isn't the first thing that springs to mind when we think about dementia, but it's this quality that paves the way for a genuine connection. One of the most important lessons I've learnt over the past year is that it's possible to connect with anyone, whichever dementia stage they're in, as long as you take the time to get to know him or her. A friend of mine, Jonas, once drew a striking analogy: 'You might hold a black belt in karate, but if you can't read your opponent, you're bound to lose.' So open up to people with dementia, don't judge them on their first response and don't contradict them, but listen and go along with what they say. Look for what they respond to, what they enjoy, and adapt, again and again. It takes a bit of time, but it's incredibly rewarding.

Jonas's father was diagnosed with Alzheimer's disease and had to go into care. Jonas told me that his father used to be very tense in the morning just before he was due to be washed. So much so that he'd cramp up, resulting in pain when moving. But then Jonas told the carers that his father loved music and that he used to wake up with it. The first time they played music, he responded immediately. The carers stayed with him while he listened, so it took a bit longer than usual to 'get started', but because he was so relaxed the bathing itself was a lot faster. The next time he visited, Jonas brought in a special playlist with his father's favourite pieces. The music was put on well before the carers came round. And the result? A totally relaxed father, who was happy to be washed. How great is that?

It really is possible to improve care by taking the time to get to know people. I know, for instance, that when you're with Ad, you should never be too forceful, or else he becomes agitated. Elly feels at ease as soon as you give her a hug. It doesn't take much for Tineke to feel redundant, and you should always greet her. Before you say something to Leny you should make eye contact and give a wave. In short: wait and see until you get a sense of what works for the other person. A genuine connection is a two-way street.

A human being

When we keep seeing the human being, he or she will never disappear. #HumanForever

A cry from the heart

My name is Teun Toebes, and I believe that people living with dementia aren't getting the attention they deserve. That makes me incredibly sad. But . . .

I'm hopeful.
And that's because of you.

Because of you I'm hopeful that the public perception
of people living with dementia is going to change for
good.
Because of you I'm hopeful for a better future
for the care of people with dementia.
Because of you I'm hopeful that everybody will start
seeing
the human being and not the illness.

Why?

THE HOUSEMATES

Because you're reading this.
Because you know that this book may be about you one
day.
And because you now know that you can change the
future.

And for that . . .
Thank you.

My friends in their own words

Now it's time for my housemates to do the talking so you can get a little glimpse into their lives. Out of respect for their experiences, all the answers have been recorded in their own words.

Name: Tineke Muschter
Date of birth: 16 May 1938
Place of birth: Utrecht
Address: Here, in this park

What do you like best about yourself?
I keep seeking out others because I don't want to be pigeonholed as an old person. I'm very patient with people, I always have been.

Are you proud of yourself?
That's a difficult question for me because there will

always be issues, but I'm reasonably proud of myself. I've done a lot for my mother and my younger brothers.

What was the best moment of your life?
Just being here, living my life for others, not just for myself.

What will you never forget?
One thing will always stay with me: when my father was deported, I was only three. I watched it happen. And I never saw my daddy again.

What's your life like now?
Very difficult at times, very challenging. And then I find myself very challenging too.

What's it like to live here?
It's important to me to belong somewhere, it still is.

Do you want to be right or happy?
Happy, because why would a person want to be right? I don't understand what's so good about that. Whenever people want to have the last word, I think to myself: what are you talking about?

MY FRIENDS IN THEIR OWN WORDS

What's your dream?
I know it sounds strange for a woman my age, but Ghanna, my dog, is the one I miss the most.

Is there anything else you'd like to say?
I'd like to thank all the people who've helped me after the loss of my nearest and dearest.

THE HOUSEMATES

Name: Leny, that's my given name. My full name is Helena Henriette. My maiden name is Kaligis, my mother and father's surname. Now I'm officially Leny de Planque, because I'm married to De Planque.
Date of birth: October 1926, an old git
Place of birth: Buitenzorg in Java, south of what was then Batavia, now Jakarta
Address: My room

What do you like best about yourself?
About myself? That I'm not infirm. That I still have arms, legs and a brain to fall back on.

Are you proud of yourself?
Average, I suppose. I know who I am. I'm proud of my parents, though, for always supporting me and giving me an education.

What was the best moment of your life?
Now there's a question. Maybe my wedding to Con de Planque. From then on, I had someone I knew I'd be faithful to and I wouldn't be all alone.

What will you never forget?
My happy childhood. My parents took good care of me. I grew up in a warm and loving home because I'm the youngest of five.

What's your life like now?
Good. I feel comfortable because everyone's nice and friendly to me. I appreciate that.

What's it like to live here?
All right, everything's fine. I've got a good life. I'm content.

Do you want to be right or happy?
Happy. It's all about having a good life with friends and family.

What's your dream?
Having a happy life with all the lovely people around me, my daughters.

Is there anything else you'd like to say?
May people live in peace. That's very important.

Name: Muriëlle, that's my first name. My middle name is Louise – a French name – and my last name is Mulier. It's written on the door
Date of birth: 1940
Place of birth: Curaçao
Address: Right now, this room, because I don't really have a home anymore

What do you like best about yourself?
My character because I never pick a fight, ever. I don't like people who think too highly of themselves because they get all puffed up. And I can't stand that. When I'm somewhere where people are quarrelling, I turn into a mouse, I hide. I don't want to take sides.

Are you proud of yourself?
Oh, yes! Of course I'm proud of myself. All people are proud of themselves, except they won't admit to it.

What was the best moment of your life?
My father used to say: 'Where's that white girl?' I had a very special relationship with him, but he's no longer with us. It's true, I was the fairest of the lot, the others were light brown. I thought it was a funny thing to say. The man had a sense of humour.

What will you never forget?
My purse.

What's your life like now?
I'm glad some of my children are still with me because one of my sons has already passed away. It's hard to lose a child.

What's it like to live here?
I miss my home. If I were granted one big wish, my immediate response would be, 'back to my house', even though I know it's impossible. You need to make your own luck here, but you don't want to be too pernickety either. I'd like to make that clear.

Do you want to be right or happy?
Both. You need to be happy if you want to keep going. And you need to trust that you're right because surely you can't stand for everything other people will have you believe?

What's your dream?
I'm eighty now and I'd like to get to ninety. That would be amazing!

Is there anything else you'd like to say?
Smile and be happy.

THE HOUSEMATES

Name: Ad van Dokkum
Date of birth: 1945, give or take a year
Place of birth: Breda
Address: Here, ward whatchamacallit

What do you like best about yourself?
I can still talk to just about anyone.

Are you proud of yourself?
Yes, because after everything I've been through, I've done all right.

What was the best moment of your life?
Getting married, of course, to Maaike. We met in a sweet shop. She was working there and I bought a big bag of sweets.

What will you never forget?
The accident at the power station in which I lost three colleagues.

What's your life like now?
You've no choice. You've no choice but to stay positive and keep going, especially now.

What's it like to live here?
At first I just sat and stared all day, but now I've got a

purpose again, and that's Ministeck. And I've got a nice room.

Do you want to be right or happy?
I'd say happy because that's something that can actually do you some good – especially at this age.

What's your dream?
To make a Ministeck painting for someone else.

Is there anything else you'd like to say?
I hope we can continue to look each other in the eye.

THE HOUSEMATES

Name: Jeanne, but you can call me Adriana
Date of birth: Before the war, but I'm not too bothered about the exact year
Place of birth: Utrecht
Address: Home

What do you like best about yourself?
Honesty, that's my top priority.

Are you proud of yourself?
I'm just an ordinary girl who's getting on a bit.

What was the best moment of your life?
Seeing my father again after he'd been shot in the war. I didn't see him for a long time and then I finally saw him in his coffin. I was only a little girl when he suddenly disappeared.

What will you never forget?
My husband's death. We had such a good family. We have a few children together.

What's your life like now?
I live for what I can do for my children, and before that my mother.

What's it like to live here?
As long as I've got enough food for the children, everything's all right.

Do you want to be right or happy?
Happiness always comes first.

What's your dream?
I hope I have a while to go yet, for the children's sake, but that's beyond my control.

Is there anything else you'd like to say?
I'd like my children to be happy and healthy.

THE HOUSEMATES

Name: My name's Eugenie
Date of birth: 4 August . . .
Place of birth: Surabaya, in Indonesia
Address: Here

What do you like best about yourself?
I can't say.

Are you proud of yourself?
I'm not proud of myself, but I'm all right.

What was the best moment of your life?
I've had many beautiful moments.

What will you never forget?
The death of my other child. It didn't have a name because it was born and then it died. That's stayed with me my whole life.

What's your life like now?
It's not bad.

What's it like to live here?
It's quite nice here.

Do you want to be right or happy?
Happiness is more important because it's not always the same.

What's your dream?
That time has passed for me.

Is there anything else you'd like to say?
Being happy is more important to me than anything else.

THE HOUSEMATES

Name: Elly Janssen
Date of birth: 22 December 1930
Place of birth: Lange Heselaan in Nijmegen
Address: Nijmegen

What do you like best about yourself?
I'm not quick to like something about myself, but it's important to me to look good. I'm often complimented on my hair, so I can't complain.

Are you proud of yourself?
Well, I don't know what to say to that. I'm not dissatisfied.

What was the best moment of your life?
Having my children and grandchildren.

What will you never forget?
Life in Nijmegen.

What's your life like now?
I like having a glass of wine with you, I always enjoy that.

What's it like to live here?
It's all right, as long as my children keep coming. They

visit me a lot and I really appreciate that. If I hadn't been a mother, my life wouldn't be as good.

Do you want to be right or happy?
Happy, what's the point in being right?

What's your dream?
For my children to be happy.

Is there anything else you'd like to say?
Don't let your tyres go flat.

Ethical considerations

Writing about life within the protected environment of a nursing home obviously comes with great responsibility.

The autonomy of people living with dementia is immensely important to me, which is why I asked my fellow residents for permission first, before I turned to their legal guardians, often their children. During or after our introductory meeting, they signed consent forms for this book.

Out of respect for my housemates, I've retained their words and perceptions, even when they couldn't have had any basis in fact. I've respected everybody's privacy, including that of my caregiver colleagues, and when people told me they didn't want to be in the book, I anonymised them and changed any identifying features.

During my very first meeting with the healthcare organisation, I singled out freedom of expression as hugely important to me. When it became clear that I was going to write *The Housemates*, I had a very open discussion with the floor manager, the communications department and the board of directors. A few months prior to publication, the staff were briefed and during a team meeting, we spoke about the experiences and emotions that resulted from my presence.

The Housemates is certainly *not* an indictment of the care sector, but of the way we perceive and deal with people living with dementia.

None of the events and anecdotes recounted here are meant as a personal reproach.

I want to be very open about the fact that in the past, in my role as a carer, I too behaved in ways that I now frown on. Not only do I regret my actions, I'll also take care not to do things that way again.

The stories in this book are all true, but I have occasionally tweaked time, place and order if I thought it would aid the narrative.

I've made every effort to be as accurate as possible when quoting facts and referencing sources. In the event of any mistakes, my apologies in advance.

Afterword
The path of most resistance

In the weeks prior to this book coming out in the Netherlands on 9 November 2021, I began to feel sick to my stomach, worried about what people would think of my work. Knowing that what I'd committed to paper wasn't the most mainstream, let alone the most popular opinion, it had taken a lot of courage to write. I told myself that whatever happened, at least my housemates' voices would be heard. From the outset, that had been one of my main motivations for writing *The Housemates*.

My fear of encountering strong opinions was only heightened by the many interviews that were beginning to fill my diary in the run-up to publication. I'm not exaggerating when I say that every day I had about three planned, with all the major national papers, radio stations and television shows. Although I'd racked up a fair amount of media experience over the years, I wasn't prepared for this eight-week whirlwind tour of the Netherlands and Belgium. When I finally retreated back to 'my' nursing home, I felt completely drained. During those two months, the outside world had marvelled at what went on in my house, but only afterwards did those 225 square feet, complete with linoleum flooring and suspended ceiling, truly feel like a safe haven.

The day before publication, I drove my old banger to The Hague, where I was to present Prime Minister Mark Rutte with the first copy. I'd met him before, after winning the Young Impact Award 2019, and he'd been vocal about his support for my work. As you'd expect from a head of government, he didn't have a lot of time, but he was really pleased that my mission had entered a new chapter. One of the first things he said was, 'I'm always mystified as to why we don't treat individuals with dementia like ordinary people.' He told me, 'I used to have a piano teacher who was clearly living with a form of dementia, and she remained not only a great instructor but also a wonderful person right until the very end.'

Just before my audience with the prime minister finished, he phoned the new minister responsible for long-term care to arrange a spontaneous visit. 'The advantage of being prime minister is that everybody always answers straightaway,' he said with a big smile on his face. With that phone call, he helped make the auspicious start to my book tour even better. 'Teun, you're an example to many, but remember, if you really want to bring about change in the world, you need to look at the smallest action with the biggest impact.' With these words of wisdom, the promise of a follow-up appointment and a warm handshake, I continued on my way to the Ministry of Health, Welfare and Sport.

The media interviews I did not only reinforced my faith in the mission, but also suggested to me that we're used to imposing change from the outside, instead of looking for ways to bring it about from within. Each and every journalist, radio host and television presenter was keen to know what new regulations I would suggest in response to my experiences at the nursing home. Hmm, regulations . . . It would appear that we're so desperate for something to hold on to that we overlook the main player in any process of transformation: ourselves. And that's understandable because when external things need fixing, that doesn't feel like a threat – more like something we can hide behind. But for me to suggest a load of new rules and regulations would mean falling into the very trap I'm trying so hard to avoid. Systems reinforce forms of exclusion and undermine self-determination, getting in the way of delivering care that is tailored to the individual.

Each year in the Netherlands, some 18 billion euros is injected into the nursing care sector, and yet I'm constantly being told that the system isn't fit for purpose because of a lack of funds. How is that possible? In the UK, £14.2 billion a year goes on social care and healthcare costs for people living with dementia.[13] Earlier this year, I visited Moldova for the documentary I am making. Many people in this Eastern European country aren't even aware of dementia; there's no money for climate-neutral nursing homes with flatscreen TVs and not every single health and safety regulation is observed when heating meals, but they do provide the warmest care I've experienced in years. Good care is not about money, but about our shared humanity.

What society and the care sector need is a renaissance, a new age of enlightenment. A change in thinking leads to a change in perspective, and a change in perspective leads to a change in behaviour. It sounds simple enough, but communicating this way of looking at things is harder than I ever imagined. Except, that is, to the people who deal directly with dementia – they feel my message in every fibre of their being. I'm still inundated with daily emails and messages on Instagram and LinkedIn from people who felt a twinge of relief after reading my book.

'Finally, someone who tells us what it's really like in a nursing home!'

'Deeply moved by your sincere words – if only my

mother had lived in your home. Instead, I could only watch as she languished. Nobody saw her for who she was. Heart-wrenching.'

'Reading your book, I can see a glimmer of hope for the care sector.'

Once they'd realised that what I was trying to say didn't involve new rules and regulations, the media and politicians were certainly interested in a fresh approach, but preferably a ready-made one that could be introduced tomorrow. The idea that a change in thinking equals a change in behaviour wasn't something they readily embraced. To their ears, it probably sounded a bit slow.

Weird as it may sound, the resistance I encountered to what I'd written about in the book confirmed to me that I'd touched a raw nerve, that this deserved a closer look. Although I repeatedly stressed that this wasn't a personal attack on care workers, but merely an observation on how we deal with individuals with dementia, I came to realise that some people did read it that way, especially those working in the sector. Like the media, they too had to get used to the fact that I wasn't fighting the traditional foe, that is to say insufficient funding, but the legacy of the welfare state and its ideas. As I experienced during my first proper driving lesson, unlearning bad habits is harder than adopting new, better ones . . .

AFTERWORD

The shift in focus from caring *for* to caring *about* is our biggest challenge. Carers have been trained in such a way that we're seen to be doing well when somebody is properly looked after according to the current standards, and we feel challenged to the core when that view is contested, when the goalposts shift. Can we really do our job differently within the existing system? What if something goes wrong? These are fine questions that take us to the heart of the matter: quality rather than quantity of life. Once we recognise that, I genuinely believe that a different outlook will no longer feel like a personal failure, but a collective gain. I'm convinced it will lead to happier relatives, carers and people with dementia, and who wouldn't want that?

During my two-and-a-half years at the nursing home, I began to see dementia as more of a social issue than a matter of care, and that's precisely why I've been able to allay carers' fears of 'not doing a good job'. The question is not whether *you* are doing a good job; my answer is always that *we* are not doing a good job. Over the years, we have created a system in which the emphasis is on safety and control and not on happiness and a sense of community. But the upside is that since we've created this system, we're also the ones who can change it, and that gives me hope.

In light of this, I began to look beyond the walls of my nursing home for ways in which we can do things differently. My search started in the Netherlands, but soon spread to other countries, because dementia recognises no borders. With an open mind, I travelled the world with friend and documentary maker Jonathan de Jong to see how other nations approach dementia and what we can learn from them. What we saw was by turns impressive, moving and beautiful. Whereas in Moldova I was gripped by the warmth and loving care, in South Korea, I saw how they were light years ahead in terms of prevention. I felt the power of community living in Africa, the open-mindedness of Scandinavian culture and experienced how people with dementia can still live life to the full in America.

Dementia is a subject that's usually spoken about in terms of loss, and yet I saw there was a world to be gained.

Een Wereld Te Winnen (A World To Win) *will be available in bookshops in the Netherlands and Belgium in late 2023*.

Notes

1   Luengo-Fernandez, R. & Landeiro, F. (in
    preparation). The Economic Burden of Dementia
    in the UK. https://dementiastatistics.org/
    statistics-about-dementia/prevalence-2/
2   Luengo-Fernandez, R. & Landeiro,
    F. (in preparation). The Economic
    Burden of Dementia in the UK. https://
    dementiastatistics.org/statistics-about-dementia/
    human-and-financial-impact/
3   Centers for Disease Control. About Dementia.
    https://www.cdc.gov/aging/dementia/index.html
4   Alzheimer's Association. Facts and Figures. https://
    www.alz.org/alzheimers-dementia/facts-figures
5   World Health Organization (15 March 2023).
    Dementia. https://www.who.int/news-room/
    fact-sheets/detail/dementia
6   World Health Organization (15 March 2023).

Dementia. https://www.who.int/news-room/
fact-sheets/detail/dementia

7 Commissie van Toezicht (2021). 'Het recht
op luchten' [The right to fresh air], www.
commissievantoezicht.nl

8 Alzheimer Nederland (2021). 'Factsheet: dementia
facts and figures', www.alzheimer-nederland.nl

9 Trouw (2021). 'Ziekteverzuim eind 2020 hoogste in
achttien jaar' [Absenteeism reaches 18-year high in
2020], www.trouw.nl

10 Nieuwsuur (2018). Interview with Dr Anne
Mei, Professor of Long-term Care and the Social
Approach to Dementia at VU Amsterdam, and
Professor Marcel Olde Rikkert, Head of Geriatrics
at Radboud UMC.

11 Alzheimer Nederland (2021). 'Levensverwachting
dementie' [Dementia life expectancy], www.
alzheimer-nederland.nl

12 Alzheimer Nederland (2021). 'Factsheet feiten en
cijfers over dementie' [Dementia: facts and figures],
www.alzheimer-nederland.nl

13 Luengo-Fernandez, R. & Landeiro,
F. (in preparation). The Economic
Burden of Dementia in the UK. https://
dementiastatistics.org/statistics-about-dementia/
human-and-financial-impact/

Acknowledgements

First of all, I want to thank the people who've taught me so much and who've changed my view of those living with dementia forever: my housemates. Dear Ad, Leny, Muriëlle, Tineke, Elly, Piet, Eugenie, Clara, Lambert, Janna, Nel, Teunie, Jeanne and Ida, I hereby solemnly promise you that I'll never forget your stories, experiences, lessons and insights. And if I can't keep my word because one day I move back into a nursing home, know that I've done everything in my power to share your stories and lessons with the world. Because you deserve that. You made the nursing home a *home* for me.

I also want to thank my nursing *home* – residential care home Voorhoeve and AxionContinu – from the bottom of my heart. I think it was incredibly brave of you to give me the chance to experience the nursing home world from the inside. Not only was it a gutsy thing to do, but it also shows that you're fully committed to a better future for care. I was allowed to live with you, and you even gave me permission to think and write *anything*, and for that, I salute you. Although most of the anecdotes come from our home, the scope of this book is ultimately much bigger. I hope that your vulnerability is an example to many, so can we get to the root of the problems and solve them together.

I'm also greatly indebted to Jonathan de Jong, for helping me write this book and for the amazing adventure we embarked on together. It's cool to see that our shared passion for improving the quality of life of people with dementia has led to this publication, as well as to a beautiful friendship. Thank you for this fine start – I can't wait to see what's next.

And let's not forget my best friend and ally, my mother. Thank you for inspiring me and for encouraging me to go on this adventure. And, of course, the same applies to my other lovely family members and relatives. A special thank you to Hans Toebes, Susan Lamers, Giel Toebes, Joep Toebes and Lieve Toebes. I love you.

Finally, I'd like to thank the people and organisations who've supported and inspired me throughout: without your help I couldn't have done any of this! Thank you, caregiver colleagues and all those in the care sector who do so much to help others every day. Thank you, Uitgeverij De Arbeiderspers, Singel Uitgeverijen and Esther Hendriks for overseeing the project and

ACKNOWLEDGEMENTS

publicising my mission. Thank you, Inge Geerdink, Margje Mahler, Francien van de Ven, Anne Mei The, Henk Nies, Wouter van Soest, Michiel van Putten, Carlo Leget, Michel van Erp, Boris van der Ham, Bas Smit, Patrick Anthonissen, Michiel de Gooijer, Juliette de Jong, Nicolette van Dam, Carin Gaemers, Olav Schuth, Zvezdan Pirtosek, Kasper Bormans, Rina Knippenberg, Marcellino Bogers, Richard Groenendijk, Pieterbas Lalleman, Jan Goddaer, Geert Bettinger, Bastus de Jong, Anke Siegers, Frans and Paula Komen, Nathalie Petersen, Hans Ubachs, Ingrid Keestra, Temitope Farombi, Cecile aan de Stegge, André de Jager, Peter Whitehouse, Jaap Bressers, Fatos Ipek, Kiki Edwards, Brenda Frederiks, Han Sol, Jetske van der Schaar, Wendy Kakebeeke, Cato de Jong and the Ministry of Health, Welfare and Sport, Actiz, PGGM, Vilans, Alzheimer Nederland, Alzheimer Europe. And finally, the media that have been following me for some time and that have been very supportive.

Thank you all!

About the author

As the eldest in a family of four, with a mother who is a nurse, care has always been part of Teun Toebes' life. So, the choice to study Higher Vocational Education nursing and Care Ethics and Policy was a logical step – the choice to work with people living with dementia was not. During a compulsory internship he was introduced to dementia care and has not been able to let go of it since.

Currently, Teun contributes to dementia care by not only observing and studying people living with dementia, but by living with them permanently on a closed ward of a nursing home. He focuses on having fun and maintaining personal contact with all his housemates to create moments of happiness and thus improve their quality of life.

Teun is the passionate co-founder and ambassador of the Article 25 Foundation. He often appears in the media and is seen as an inspiring face of dementia care in Europe. Teun has won several awards for his work and initiatives, strengthening his mission to make dementia care more humane worldwide.

@teuntoebes
teuntoebes.com
article25foundation.com